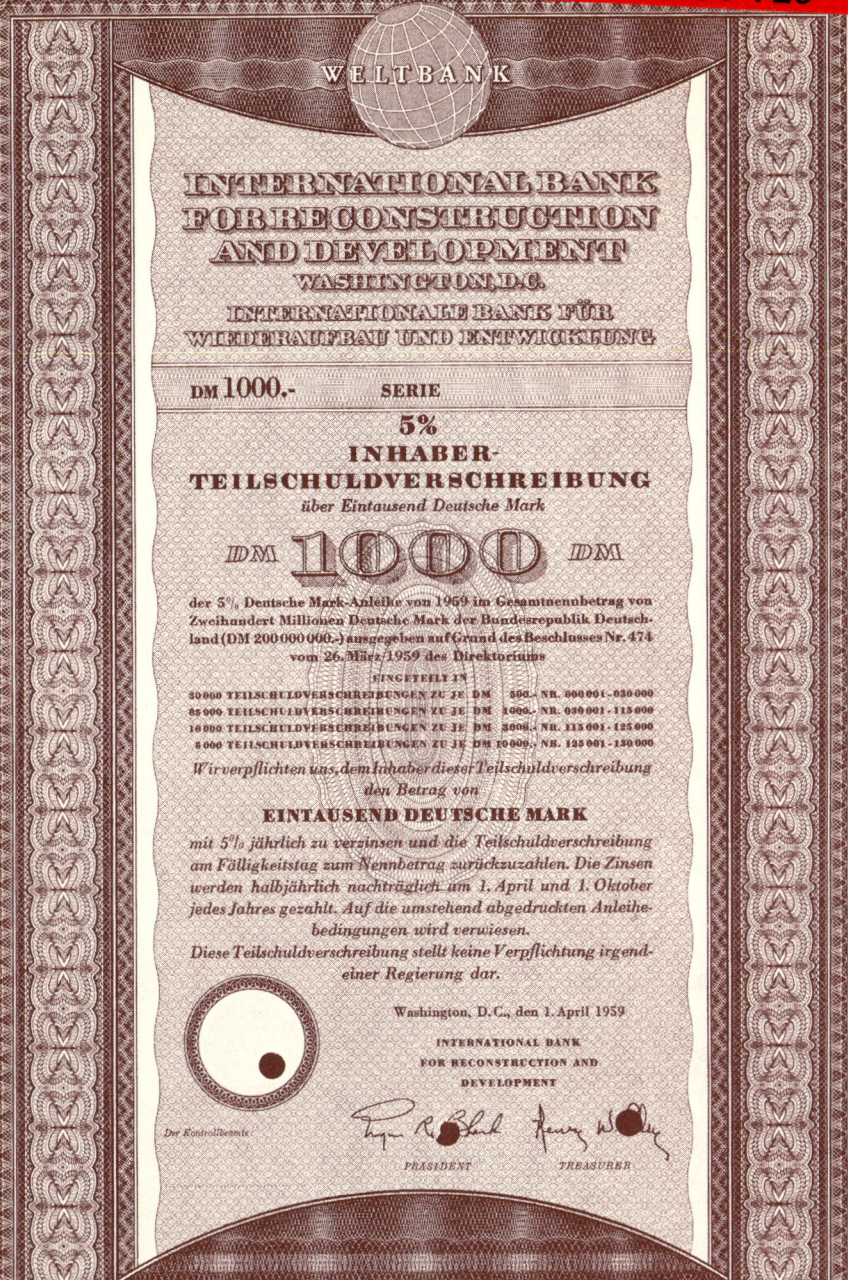

Also by James Morris

AS I SAW THE U.S.A.

THE HASHEMITE KINGS

ISLAM INFLAMED: A MIDDLE EAST PICTURE

SOUTH AFRICAN WINTER

SULTAN IN OMAN

THE WORLD OF VENICE

THE ROAD
TO HUDDERSFIELD

A Journey to Five Continents

THE ROAD TO HUDDERSFIELD

A Journey to Five Continents

BY

JAMES MORRIS

NEW YORK
PANTHEON BOOKS
A Division of Random House

FIRST PRINTING

© Copyright, 1963, by James Morris
All rights reserved under International and Pan-American Copyright Conventions. Published in New York by Pantheon Books, a division of Random House, Inc.
Manufactured in the United States of America
by The Haddon Craftsmen, Inc., Scranton, Pa.
Library of Congress Catalog Card Number: 63-7350

DESIGN BY HERBERT H. JOHNSON

Author's Note

THIS book about the World Bank was commissioned by the World Bank, but it is in no sense an advertisement or apologia. I was left entirely free to travel where I liked, and I have been at pains to record every criticism of the Bank that I have ever heard. I was invited to write the book as an engineer might be invited to build a bridge, and every detail of its construction, from the stresses to the sometimes gaudy paintwork, is all mine.

Many people, however, have helped me with the job, and I must particularly thank two members of the Bank's staff. The first is Mr. Harold Graves, the wittiest of critics, who once observed of a particularly wild misstatement in the manuscript that it was "a genuine curiosity, like a whelk with a left-handed spiral." The other is Mr. Eugene Black, toward whom I have neither wish nor need to be sycophantic, but who seems to me an almost perfect patron of what might at a pinch be considered the arts.

Author's Note

Mr. Black has now retired from the presidency of the Bank, and has handed over to Mr. George D. Woods: but his tenure of office was so long, he stamped his personality so strongly upon the institution, and he remains so clearly responsible for its present pattern, that I have preferred to describe it as it was during the last weeks of his presidency, at the beginning of 1963. It was Black's Bank then, and so it must long remain —if not in the textbooks, at least in the world's memory.

J. M.

Contents

1 Huddersfield—the taste for change—processes of revolution—money—rival sugar-daddies—tumult of philanthropy—a heavy paragon — 1

2 A funny place—origins and aims—how it works—the clearinghouse—Eugene Black—criticisms—qualities—dams, pipes, and newsprint—"At least He's consistent" — 35

3 Weird monarchy—pastoral integrity—Berghida—despotisms and discontents—omens of Huddersfield—bankers' yeast—too fast—L equals $\dfrac{rRP-(t+t')L}{i}$ — 75

4 Yanhee—the lotus country—readier than most—why?—impulses to change—in the dam's gift—doubts—pains to come—"a pity" — 109

5 Improper conduct—the two Italies—the Cassa—reputation of the south—obstacles to progress—on the move—Scopello — 135

Contents

6 On geography—the other Athens—malaise—geographical grimace—the Magdalena—period piece—meaning of a railroad—Tequendama   169

7 The Punjab—aftermaths of empire—the Garden of India—partition—eight years' talk—the treaty—at Attock   197

8 Still studying—shortage of clients—liberal tendencies—IDA—plastic Zion?—back to Huddersfield—a comfort to end with   223

Plates

Following page 112

I   *The World Bank, Washington*
(PHOTO: WORLD BANK)

II   *Halifax, Yorkshire*
(PHOTO: RADIO TIMES HULTON PICTURE LIBRARY)

III   *Ethiopian Village*
(PHOTO: PAUL ALMASY)

IV   *Sukkar Barrage, Indus River, Pakistan*
(PHOTO: WORLD BANK)

V   *Cefalu, Sicily*
(PHOTO: RADIO TIMES HULTON PICTURE LIBRARY)

VI   *Siam: A floating market on one of the crowded Bangkok canals*
(PHOTO: B.O.A.C.)

VII   *Atlantic Railroad, Colombia*
(PHOTO: UNITED NATIONS)

Maps

Areas of operations   40–41

Ethiopia   81

Siam   115

Southern Italy   141

Colombia   175

The Indus Basin   203

I

*Huddersfield, the taste for change,
processes of revolution,
money, rival sugar-daddies,
tumult of philanthropy,
a heavy paragon*

CROUCHED in a declivity among the Yorkshire moors, in the harsh allure of the Brontë country, there lies the town of Huddersfield: and in that foursquare earthy English borough, a place of drab and fusty reputation, this book properly and symbolically begins.

It is not guides or hotel reservations that you will need if ever you make the pilgrimage to those stark smoke-filled valleys, but a responsive sense of history, for Huddersfield's fascination is more evocative than architectural: her passport to Baedeker is the fact that here, in these grim moorlands of northern England, the technical revolution began—a historical convulsion so fierce and inflammatory that it has changed half the world already, and is now tumultuously transforming the rest. All around you, as you stand at the top of Chapel Hill, you may see the monuments of that tremendous but brutal event which erupted among the Yorkshire hill farms a couple of centuries ago: the long huddle of the textile mills, creeping away to the moor's edge; the marching file of tall brick chimneys, their vapors drifting into the dusk; the coveys

The Road to Huddersfield:

of cramped terrace houses, jammed hugger-mugger against the hillsides; the dingy red brick everywhere, the patina of dirt, labor, and middle age. It is not, at first sight, an exuberant scene. The wind blows chill and bluff off Wessenden. The buses lumber sadly by to Leeds and Slaithwaite, Oldham and Crosland Moor, housewives in kerchiefs peering wanly out of their misted windows. The evening sky is gray and melancholy. Somewhere a steam locomotive blows its lonely whistle, and there is a distant clanging of couplings in a freight yard.

Here nevertheless, in the Huddersfields of the north, our modern world was born. These horny, stocky, taciturn people were the first to live by chemical energies, by steam, cogs, iron, and engine grease, and the first in modern times to demonstrate the dynamism of the human condition. This is where, by all the rules of heredity, the sputnik and the moon rocket were conceived. Baedeker may not recognize it, but this is one of history's crucibles. Until the start of the technical revolution, in the second half of the eighteenth century, England was an agricultural country, only vestigially invigorated by the primitive industries of the day. She was impelled, for the most part, by muscular energies—the strong arms of her islanders, the immense shaggy legs of her noble Shire horses. She was already mining coal and smelting iron, digging canals and negotiating bills of exchange, and she had long since moved out of the subsistence stage, when men grow food simply to feed themselves. Agriculture itself had changed under the impact of new ideas: the boundless open fields of England had almost all been enclosed, and lively farmers were experimenting with crop rotations, breeding methods, and winter feed. There was a substantial merchant class already, fostered by trade and adventure, and a solid stratum of literate yeomen.

For most ordinary people, though, in most everyday ways, England remained more or less the kind of country she had been a century before, her affairs still rigidly geared to the production and exchange of foodstuffs. Her landowners were rich and cultivated, her peasantry was ignorant and obsequious, and most of her people lived in the country. It was not a feudal society but a paternal one, a land of squires, cultured country parsons, the tugging of forelocks, and the dispensation of old folk remedies by tender-hearted gentlefolk, a country of such gentle pastoralism that a French nobleman visiting England in 1784 described her as "the finest country in Europe, for variety and verdure, for beauty and richness, for rural neatness and elegance—a feast for the sight, a charm for the mind." In this green and placid place the memories of one generation were very like the memories of the one before. No new source of power had been discovered for centuries, no new method of transportation, no vital new mercantile commodity. The pattern of patrician, pleb, and tradesman was so precisely etched, and the forms of good behavior were so generally accepted, that life had an almost tribal flavor to it, unquestioning and secure. Only the medication of religion, it was thought in those days, could much change the world. Physically its form was molded once and for all, and the general arrangement of affairs, the relationships between the classes, the disparities between rich and poor—these things were divinely ordained and could be improved only by prayer and chaste living, if at all. History shifted, to be sure: empires were won and lost, battles were fought in remote oceans, great men rose and toppled; but in the way common people lived, ate, and moved about, England had not much changed from one era to another. A medieval resident of Oxford, say, returned to the city in Queen Anne's day, would find it all familiar enough. Indeed, since the departure of the Romans, nobody had thought of having central heating, and it is said that the chariots of the Legions rattled from Londinium to Eboracum a good deal faster than George III's mail coaches from London to York.

Science changed all this, together with money. It was a process long in gestation, with its seeds far back in the New Learning of the Middle Ages, the inquiries of the Renaissance, and the audacities of the Reformation; but with the opening puffs of the steam age, the English realized almost with a start that a way of life need not be sacrosanct, even without the divine intervention. Diffidently at first, robustly later, with a flood of new ideas, new inventions, and new enterprises, they set in motion all those processes of change and development that were to transform their society from bucolic calm to brass-bound industry. Gradually it transpired that the new natural sciences, first probed by the savants of the eighteenth century, could be employed to make men richer and theoretically happier, to set a whole nation afire, to shift its entire outlook on human satisfaction, to give it such a shot in the arm or kick in the pants that it would never be remotely the same again.

Some say a decline of religion contributed to this new vision, that as men turned away disillusioned from the promise of future salvation, they savagely turned their attention to saving themselves there and then. Others maintain that only the newly crystallized notion of nationalism, with its concomitants of unity and State purpose, could have inspired such an extraordinary jolt of attitudes. Certainly the widening horizons of trade, empire, and settlement must have induced men to look beyond the cramped and static boundaries of their parochial origins. But whatever the metaphysical causes, however complex the historical stimuli, it was pre-eminently steam and hard cash that actually ignited the technical revolution: steam, because it came like a miracle after eons of muscle energy, powering the new factories and binding the whole nation with railroads: cash, because only shrewdly organized investment could provide the base for such sensational risks and leaps in the dark (for to this revolution, as to all others, there were powerful elements of roguery, eccentricity, and bravado).

Science and money did it, bolstered always by ruthlessness. It was no lily road to well-being. Modern England was made in half a century, as you can see up there in Yorkshire. Wherever you look, there are the mills and tenements of the revolution—faded now and crumbling, or patched up with concrete and chromium, but still keenly suggestive of an old and furious momentum. The sheer scale of it all—the speed and energy with which the railroads were built, the rivers harnessed, the moorland valleys clothed in masonry—is astonishing to contemplate even now, and could only have been achieved by an impetus of violent force and brutality. It was not merely a matter of building factories; it involved the shattering of old shibboleths, the re-examination of old values, the migration of thousands of people from gentle countryside to raw new town. "At the corner of Wood Street" Wordsworth's poor

The Road to Huddersfield:

Susan used to pause: and from that dismal spot she would see, as in a vision, a glimpse of her lost rural England:

> ... *a single small cottage, a nest like a dove's,*
> *The one only dwelling on earth that she loves.*

Some good, wise men contributed to the fizz of those years, but the first of the Yorkshire industrialists were seldom sensitive people. They were self-made, half-educated, vigorous, bullying, irrepressible men of ambition, always pushing, always grasping, edging ever more insistently into a society dominated till then by men of a gentler breeding. They made their money partly by brave initiative but partly by the heartless exploitation of simple folk: it was the *entrepreneurs* who invested the money, sustaining the pace and vigor of it all, but it was the working people who provided it, by accepting far lower wages than they were worth. Factory conditions were appalling. Housing was often repulsive. The treatment of child workers was one of the disgraces of European history, and the Dickensian squalor of the new industrial England, with all its cracked values and discarded traditions, survives to this day, not only in slums and points of view, but even in bone structures. In many a North Country town you may still sometimes observe, in the figures of elderly passers-by, the rickety legs, bowed shoulders, and pinched physiques that were the price of a nation's progress.

All this you may sense in Huddersfield, the Oderesfelte of the Saxons. Scarcely a trace remains there of the old pastoral England, the hunting parsons and the cottage retainers. Its gentry has long sold out and vanished, its fragments of half-timber are swamped in Victorian Gothic, its medieval traditions are overlaid, its country origins quite forgotten. You can see the open moorland from Chapel Hill running away to Flockton or Todmorden like a dream of release beyond the chimney stacks, but seldom was a town more intensely urban: for the catalyst of industry is aciduous indeed, and the old historical roots soon rot away in its intensity. Everywhere there are echoes of old miseries. To this day the trade unions retain a stubborn militancy that is a relic of old ill-treatment. To this day the local motorcycle club calls itself "The Luddites," after those poor, angry, bewildered folk who, baffled alike by science and by economics, smashed up the new-fangled machines of those valleys in an orgy of dazed resentment. To this day the stunted terrace houses (Violet Street and Lily Street, Hope Street and Berry Brow) crouch quaintly but damply back to back, instinct with rheumatism, mothers-in-law, and strong, sweet tea. To this day you may feel, in the faceless factory alleys of this place, the barren materialism of the pioneers—careless of everything beautiful, and soft, and old, and useless. Huddersfield is a town without grace: she is, to adopt a local tailors' classification, of a "short and portly" style. In her streets you may easily imagine the harshness of the original technical revolution, and you can hardly escape the relics of its gusto. It was a brave paradox that led the visionary Blake, summoning his arrows of desire, to envisage the new Jerusalem among those dark satanic mills.

The Huddersfields were the pace-makers, but today there is scarcely a nation of the earth that does not wish to follow them down the highway to the mills. Despite a few wan rearguard actions, from romantics or tourist associations, the world almost universally accepts the proposition that the machine way is the right way, and that change is not merely possible and desirable, but actually inevitable. One by one the States are reaching the particular point in their history that the British reached two centuries ago when they burst into the effulgence of their steam and brass. For every people it is a cathartic moment of vision, of new awareness, never satisfactorily defined. It has been called the revolution of rising expectations—when a people realizes at last that life may actually be expected to improve. It has been called an illumination of choices—when it dawns upon a society that history is not preordained, that a tribe may choose another chiefly family or even do without a chief at all. It has been likened to the takeoff of an aircraft—when a national economy develops enough power to get it off the ground at last and thereafter keep it moving with ever-increasing acceleration. It has been analyzed more as the moment when a nation learns to apply savings and science methodically to the earning of man's daily bread.

For myself, I prefer simply to collate these several stages or shelves of history with Huddersfield herself, for in the emergent nations of today, each groping or storming toward its own technical revolution, you may recognize all the symptoms of that old changing England: the cruelty and the excitement, the hope and the pathos, the abandonment of old ideals and the festive acceptance of new, the throttling of the past and the exaltation of the future. To grasp the nature of the relationship between poor and rich, ignorant and enlightened, among the simpler peoples today, try looking closely at one of those eighteenth-century prints of English mansions drawn in the heyday of English pastoralism. There stands the great house, elaborate in formal gardens, with the gentlefolk stylish on their horses in the paddock, and the ladies scented in their bowers, and outside the high brick walls the carts of the peasantry trundling along rutted tracks. If you work your imagination a little, envisage the dust that swirled around those cart wheels, and the lofty isolation of the squire, and the diseased illiteracy of the carter, and the patient poverty that lay beyond the picture frame. If you think about the scene for a moment or two, you will realize that the elegant pre-industrial England of the periwigs and the landscape gardens had a good deal in common with the Afghanistans, say, the Ethiopias, or perhaps the Burmas of today. Such is the measure of a Huddersfield revolution and its effect upon a nation's character.

There is, however, one fundamental difference. In the early days of English industrialization, only the seers or the moguls saw what it would mean in terms of money, creature comfort, excitement. Today the simplest rustic on the hay wagon has at least an inkling of what lies over the garden wall. Ours is a world of obtrusive contrasts, from modern to antique, television screen to mud hovel, vulgar to fastidious—anomalies so pungent and so ubiquitous that contrast provides a leitmotif for almost every modern travel book. In Cairo, to choose a particularly glaring example of the genre, it is only a ten-cent bus ride from a medieval back street, alive with sorcerers, circumcisers, and superstitions, to all the neon glitter of Shepheard's, Groppi's, and Conrad Hilton. In the markets of west Africa, you may still find, stubbornly ensconced among the nylons, the chicken livers, dried monkey heads, rats' claws, and fetuses of the witch doctors. In Arabia, convertible is yoked lopsidedly

The Road to Huddersfield:

with camel. In southern Italy, the man beside you in the espresso bar may well share his living room with a cow. Even the superb restaurants of France are supplied by the labors of an archaic and often secretive peasantry. Fifty years ago travelers seldom wrote of contrast as they moved in pomaded splendor from temple yard to pyramid: today it is this feeling of ironic confrontation, sometimes tragic, sometimes only comical, that most impresses the wandering observer and sends him dizzy and bemused in search of synonyms. All the pressures of politics and propaganda, too, reinforce this sense of imbalance. It has been said that Hollywood, with its glittering caricatures of how the rich live, has been the most compulsive of revolutionary forces: and so universal has been the contagion that even in fatalist Asia the pursuit of happiness is now recognized as a valid political aim, not just a spiritual exercise.

And happiness comes, they nearly all say, out of a factory chimney. Almost everyone nowadays, from the loftiest sheik to the most bestial backwoods primitive, has felt some backwash of modernity, if it is only a blown bulb discarded by some passing alpinists, or a tin of baked beans from a sergeant's messkit, and there is an irrepressible urge among the simpler nations of the earth to possess their own steel mills, computers, and pit-head baths. Technical revolution is seen as the universal panacea, and few peoples nowadays are prepared to honor the traditional disciplines of society—wisdom and generosity for the rich man, respectful labor for the poor. Sometimes the urge to change is only an expression of foolish national pride, to be satisfied by vainglorious gestures. Sometimes it is an ill-conceived desire, engendered by generations of foreign rule or patronage, to stand all alone in the world, self-sufficient and self-employed. Sometimes it is politics, smoky circuses for insufficient bread. Sometimes it is scarcely more than a yearning for fun (life in a primitive pastoral village can be excruciatingly monotonous if once your appetite has been whetted for jazzier pleasures). Sometimes it is the result of urgent and awful pressures: poverty, wasting natural assets, an explosive increase in population. Sometimes it is no more or less than an irresistible historical process, the fulfillment of one era, the opening of another—the intuitive public certainty that a community has reached the peak or nadir of its old system and must now start afresh.

Most of the experts agree, too, that the purely agricultural societies are rightly doomed, and that the impetus of economic development must be toward new industries, new sources of power, a spread of urban living. Here and there a farming people like the Danes may survive if they are advanced and sophisticated enough: but only industry, say the pundits, can absorb the world's surplus manpower and keep this planet in the requisite condition of economic expansion. For myself, though I must perforce accept their statistics, I still have doubts. I do not trust the judgment of economists, and I wonder whether something fundamental is not drained from the human spirit as the green places vanish, one by one, and contact with nature is confined to oxygen tubes and television screens. Anyone with a sneaking sympathy for the thesis that experts are wrong, people are impossible, and all progress is for the worse—anyone of simmering traditionalist tendencies must view with some disquiet the philosophies of universal modernity. So much that is brash, heartless, and ugly stems from too sharp and unthinking a change of tradition. The uneasy hybrid

The Road to Huddersfield:

cultures of Africa are one example; another is the appalling rate of tooth decay among English schoolchildren, whose parents, suddenly hoisted into industrial affluence, squander their high wages heedlessly on candy and gewgaws.

The trust in change, though, is inescapable, and is often exceedingly moving. I was once wandering alone in the highlands above La Paz, the alpine capital of Bolivia, when I met a raggedy old cowherd in a high grazing ground on the edge of the snow (where he was guarding four young bulls destined for the city bull rings). He was the simplest kind of Andean Indian, wearing a queer sort of skullcap with earflaps and looking as knobby and wind-roughened as an old juniper. When I approached him, I saw that his right eye was bleary, swollen, and wet with tears. Some weeks before, he told me, a particle of grain had lodged beneath the eyelid, and now it was puffy and septic. And, edging up close to me, looking up at me with his good eye and summoning a wan, quivering smile, that old man invited me with absolute heart-rending confidence to cure him, so sure was he that the mere breath of modern man, like the antique touch of royalty, could dispel such rural miseries.

No wonder the yearning for progress is so irresistible. It may only show in an anxious eye, a dog-eared picture book, a squinted peer through your field glasses (in Nepal they still believe that binoculars enable the westerner to see beneath the crust of the earth, where the rubies and emeralds lie). It may be expressed more tragically in the inexorable movement of poor people everywhere from countryside to city, from thatched cottage to suburban maisonette, from barn to assembly line. The awful slums of South America, huddled among the sybaritic delights, are only an echo of Poor Susan's reverie, and so are the degradations of Calcutta railroad station, where the starving migrants lie about in hundreds wrapped in rags and newspaper. The romantic view of pastoral living is almost confined to artistic amateurs, as any honest farm laborer will robustly assure you if you are fool enough to compliment him upon the peace and quiet. A yearning for solitude and open spaces is not one of the commoner impulses of humanity, and the ideal of serene poverty, though still cherished by sophisticates and ascetics, is generally as discredited as Rousseau's vision of the noble savage. The desire for weekend cottages comes late in a society's lurching progress toward utter urbanity: before you feel the need to retreat into the country, you usually feel the need to escape into the slums.

The simpler half of our contemporary world, then, with its eyes on the rockets and refrigerators of the sophisticated half, is hoping always to modernize itself; and, indeed, by and large the difference between a rich nation and a poor one is the difference between a mechanical and a muscular society. Before the Industrial Revolution in England, living standards were very much the same everywhere; today it can perhaps be said that a third of the world has passed the Huddersfield crossroads into industrial prosperity, and the other two thirds is, by one route or another, straining to get there. In the past the process has never been easy, whatever the means. It has often been painful and sometimes violent, more like childbirth than menopause.

Western Europe industrialized itself more or less in the British way, a little later for political, social, or educational

The Road to Huddersfield:

reasons, but generally employing the same techniques of investment and inducement. The North Americans built their Pittsburghs and Detroits by the often uncompromising exploitation of poor immigrant labor—men who were prepared to work almost any hours, for almost any wage, in almost any conditions, for the chance of eventual dignity. The Japanese, alone in Asia, modernized their ancient kingdom by a paradoxical combination of fierce traditional discipline, a genius for adaptation, and a vast diligent labor force. The Russian Communists, continuing a technical revolution that their Tsarist forebears had already begun, transformed their society from feudalism to industrial supremacy by methods of murderous coercion. It was never easy. In every instance, it required a strong central government and a stable political structure; at least the nucleus of an educated class, with some knowledge of management as well as technique; what the economists call an infrastructure of roads, railways, telegraphs, and ports; a ruthless determination not to be hampered by the traditions of the past, whether they were represented by faithful nannies or miraculous icons; a hard core of reasonably efficient and relatively incorrupt institutions, from post offices to patents boards; and, not least, the readiness to risk and save money, public or private.

Sometimes it was achieved, as in America, by the full armory of private enterprise, concerned less with national prestige than with personal profit. Sometimes, as in Russia, it was above all the State that fathered the process, seeing in it a promise not merely of prosperity but also of power. To men of all political creeds, in the century after Huddersfield, mechanization became a symbol of fruition. The Stalinist film-makers had tractors for heroes; the Model T Ford was the very emblem of The American Way; and as for the British themselves, so well did the machine age suit them that by 1913, when their population was 40 million, their overseas investments were worth more than all the rest of the world's put together, and were almost as valuable, in real terms, as those possessed by the United States, 180 million strong, half a century later. In peace, it was the massive security of Victoria's Britain that spoke loudest for Huddersfield; in war, it was perhaps the astonishing victory achieved by the Japanese over the Russians in the war of 1901, proof positive that out of technique comes triumph.

For the eager young nations of today, the task of modernization is in some ways easier than it was for the pioneers. For one thing, it has been amply demonstrated that anyone can do it; for another, a kind of initial deposit of modernity was often laid by those vast empires which, until a couple of decades ago, divided most of the pastoral world among themselves. Technically the transition from muscle to machine is no longer really difficult, given some degree of literacy, enough money, a modicum of help from abroad, and plenty of time. Machines are easy enough to come by, managers can be hired, boys can be sent for training in Moscow or in Massachusetts, a good engineer will build you a road, a dam, or a railroad line in any terrain on earth. Constructing a modern mechanized society is no longer a job for visionaries, whether a State chooses to do it by compulsion (like China) or persuasion (like India).

You have only to look at the automatic telephone exchange in Addis Ababa, a miracle of delicate connections that has been assembled by Ethiopian technicians, to know that the state of a society, let alone the color of a skin, no longer impedes the progress of technical knowledge. India is, I suppose, one of the most ramshackle and unwieldy of States, yet her steel mills are now admirably efficient. Ghana is one of the most unprepossessing of republics, incorrigibly snarled up in personal ambition and immaturities, but the usual academic standard of university students in Accra is higher than the British average. The Arab of the desert is a figure of birdlike inconsequence, evasion, and charm, only one generation removed from the camel raids and the blood feuds, yet no freckled American youth is better able, with an inch of wire and a gob of chewing gum, to revive an exhausted automobile. It takes time, and in the end the debilitations of climate may win after all; but no initial magic is needed nowadays to turn a yokel into a machine man.

The legacy of imperialism contributes to this quickening of abilities, if only because resentment often sharpens the senses. Most of the aspirant States of today are ex-colonies or, like the South American republics, countries that have recently detached themselves from the leading strings of more experienced Powers. Before and between the two wars a groundwork of industrialization was laid in many countries by the agents of foreign domination, political or economic. In the heyday of British supremacy, fifty separate organizations were all at work in London promoting overseas investment, and almost the whole financial structure of South America was established, in the century after that continent's emancipation, by foreign enterprise: in Argentina, for example, the British alone were responsible for the first steamship, the first wire fence, the first sheep-dip, the first gas, the first electric light, the first meat-packing plant, the first insurance company, the first banks, streetcars, telephones, and railroads, not to mention the first games of polo, soccer, tennis, golf, and rugby football.

For several decades, impelled by motives sometimes honorable, sometimes shifty, sometimes deluded, sometimes farsighted, the imperial Powers of western Europe poured money into their dependent territories of Africa and Asia, and into the temperate zones of South America. It was not often that they established manufacturing industries in those parts to compete with their own factories at home. However, they did organize the extraction and preparation of raw materials. They did throw the roads and railways across those distant landscapes. In some territories they fostered the incipient educated middle classes that must provide the skills of management today. Here and there they founded civil services of an excellence that still survives. They provided, for most of the time, that basis of public order which, whatever its moral or political implications, is the first essential of development. We would be hypocritical to be effusive about their altruism, but blind to ignore their achievements. Largely because of imperialism, there are few countries in the world today that have not tasted some physical benefits of the technical civilization, whether it be dinner on the Bombay Mail or a tetanus shot in the Congo.

Metaphysically it is a different story. In literacy, in culture, in skills, in experience, in understanding of money and means, in popular attitudes, in public integrity, in maturity, most of today's emergent countries are still centuries behind eighteenth-century England, that "feast for the sight and charm for the mind," which at the moment of Huddersfield had not only produced great poets and statesmen by the dozen but Newton, Locke, Hume, and a whole gallery of eminent mathematicians, philosophers, and political economists. England was already a complete civilized State, an experienced maritime and commercial Power. Her successors today are trying to leap direct from backward dependency to complete scientific sovereignty—sometimes from the Middle Ages to the nuclear age. Occasionally you may find a colonial territory so soaked in European custom, so integrated with the suzerain Power, that all the attitudes of modernity are there already, only waiting to be sparked. Martinique, for example, away in the splendor of the Caribbean, alive with bobbing straw hats, blazing exotic flowers, rum, and perpetual sunshine, is so deeply infused with everything French, from Marie-Claire patterns to archeological societies, that though there is scarcely a citizen of the island who could confidently be classed as white, nevertheless the island's reactions, postures, and aspirations are as mature and moderate as anything in Europe.

Elsewhere, though, the aspirant nations are seldom so restrained, seldom so sophisticated, and there is often an undeniable streak of pique or pride to their hankering after modernism. The poor world of today ranges from great and ancient cultures to pocket States of Balkan fragmentation, only a flag's length from the trees. But when we think about the contemporary technical revolution, erupting simultaneously if erratically all over the globe, we must remember that it is happening sometimes to societies roughly equivalent, in frame of mind and degree of worldly experience, to Europe five or six centuries ago. In South America there are countless peasants who have flown in airplanes before they have set eyes on a tarred road: so shattering are the transitions of our time, and so easy has it become to skip a historical stage or two in the headlong pursuit of progress.

Without much discrimination, contemporary history judges that all these States, from the noble to the footling, are ripe for the great change—ready to move from purely agricultural, subsistence economies into the kind of world that lives by buying and selling, by making things and putting things together. Indeed, the truth is that history has no choice. The birth rate now exceeds the death rate so dramatically that every minute the world's population increases by sixty souls and by the end of this century may well have doubled. (Friday, November 13, 2026, was recently forecast by a University of Illinois research team as Doomsday, the moment when, if things continue as they are, the population of the world will squeeze itself into nemesis.) Already the earth is running short of arable land, and it becomes clearer every day that mankind can survive, like Frankenstein, only by the abilities of the machine. But more than all this, history can only recognize the inflexible will of the poor peoples to live like the richer half—the Huddersfield way. Nothing on the planet today is more vital and inflammatory than this eagerness of the aspirant peoples, their burning desire for change and opportunity.

The most obvious thing they need is money. Indeed, some economists tend to melt the whole process down to hard cash. What turns a traditional society into a modern one, they say, is pre-eminently a high enough rate of investment—production instead of mere consumption. The British financed their original technical revolution out of the profits of empire and a slow, orderly mercantile development. The Americans financed theirs largely by raising money abroad. (By the end of the nineteenth century European investors had sunk $3,700,000,000 in the United States.) The Russians did it, after the revolution, by means of Communist economics so savage or topsy-turvy that they could switch consumption into production by the merest flick of a commissar's pen, or summon a few million rubles out of the steppes by the sheer exertion of dogma.

Today's aspirant countries usually have no such ready resources. Some of them, to be sure—like Ghana, Malaya, or Peru—have immense natural advantages, and are sustained by the market for raw materials. Others, though—like Jordan or Pakistan—seem to have almost no way of earning their keep at all, no apparent means of ever improving their own affairs. (They say that just as the bumblebee is aerodynamically incapable of flying, so the Republic of Lebanon is an economic impossibility.) Others again—like Egypt or India—though vast and productive by most standards, are faced with such appalling conundrums of birth rate, poverty, and hunger that all their exertions, all their sacrifices seem to leave them more or less where they were before—working a hopeless treadmill to maintain the status quo. In some countries rich men are unwilling to sink their money into industry, preferring the old security of land ownership, or lending it to smaller agriculturists at dizzy rates of profit. (An old acquaintance of mine in Chile told me blandly upon inquiry that he earned his living nowadays by lending out small sums of money at 90% interest.) In other parts of the world, though the potential of the industrial way is clearly understood, somehow local investors prefer to put their faith in Swiss, American, or West German concerns, rather than risk their money, as good patriots should, in Wulustan Textile, Mineral, and General Development Corporation, Inc.

Few countries, therefore, can now achieve a technical revolution without money from abroad. China is perhaps the only contemporary exception. To buy a ticket to Huddersfield, you need a rich uncle somewhere. This implies a phenomenal strain upon the capital resources of the rich countries, for the scale of the demand is enormous, so sudden has been the new understanding that has followed two world wars and the collapse of the imperial system. It is indeed hard to know when a country is over the industrial hump or when you can define a State as rich or poor, simple or sophisticated. Is Russia, with her immense backward regions, a *developed* country? Or South Africa, with her towering cities and her rock-bottom African reserves? Or Ireland, in some ways a State of extreme urbanity, in others stagnantly backward? Even the States of western Europe, the most subtly civilized of all, still welcome infusions of foreign cash. If we take Huddersfield as our yardstick, we can reckon that perhaps two thirds of the world is poor and aspirant: two thirds of the world, mostly in the tropical zones, urgently demands modernization—that is to say, in this particular context, hard cash. And if two thirds of the world justifiably needs money, only the other third can supply it.

Before World War II, money for developing countries

generally came from imperial stocks, from private investment, or from government loans. In those untidy and inconclusive years, many a rash investor singed his well-manicured fingers. The imperialists, notably British or French, discovered that empires were not, by and large, paying propositions. It is an ironic fact that the British and French economies ceased to expand with any gusto at the very period when, toward the end of the nineteenth century, they became full-blown, wholehog imperialists in the modern sense; and, conversely, Englishmen were never so prosperous as they have been since the sun set on their white man's burden. Private investors often flourished—as you may see from many a Guatemalan banana grove, Argentinian packing plant, shoe factory in India, or copper mine in Rhodesia; but they suffered, too, from the chronic instability of many a quarrelsome and avaricious backwoods State, and from the dismal cycle of slump and boom that plagued the era. It was an unhappy period for international finance. Often loans were brutally repudiated. More often still, they went by default. (In 1933, 37% of all loans to foreign governments outstanding on the New York market were in default.) The Finns were the only people in Europe who repaid their 1914 war debts to the United States on time and in full. The appalling inconsistencies of South American finance, displayed in innumerable welshings, backslidings, and procrastinations, have colored North American attitudes to this very day, and make many a Wall Street mogul blanch and crack his knuckles when confronted with the very suggestion of Brazil.

Since the last war the situation has radically changed. In 1939 half the earth was ruled by the European empires, who usually seemed to think, for reasons later proved mistaken, that they would gain by preserving their dominions as national enclaves, providing raw materials, markets, and opportunities alike for their own business people. Little foreign investment or enterprise was encouraged in those vast subject territories. The ruling powers were scarcely eager to establish manufacturing industries in their colonies. (To this day you may still find some opposition in Huddersfield to the modernization of primitive States, in the past such contented customers for beads, baubles, and piece goods.) In any case, canny financiers generally preferred to invest their funds in empty temperate countries, rather than teeming tropical ones.

Today, though, the empires are released and fragmented, and each emancipated State is clamoring for its own technical revolution—together with many an older nation, shaken out of its habitual apathy by the rip-roaring stimulation of the times. There is an insatiable demand for money to hasten the leveling of the world, the bridging of the gap between the almost obscenely affluent West and the almost sickeningly destitute remainder. Almost the whole of Africa, South America, and Asia fizzles with the revolution of rising expectations, which leaves, in effect, Europe and North America to satisfy it. And if you would measure the gap between the two, bear in mind that the volume of external trade in Canada is just seventy times as great as the volume of trade in that Shangri-La of old Africa, Ethiopia.

This is a different order of things from the sporadically developing world of the thirties; but by one means and another the demand for money has usually been met. There has been a shortage of private capital since the last war, as

The Road to Huddersfield:

the advanced Powers themselves have reorganized their industries out of chaos; but, by any previous standards, there has been a regular torrent of public funds pouring into the simpler countries. Some have benefited from the capital accumulated by the neutrals during the war. Some have been drawing ever since upon the sterling debts piled up by Britain's vanished fleets and armies. Most of the cash has inevitably come, however, from the United States of America, sometimes for reasons of noble simplicity—the happiness of one State contributes to the welfare of all others—sometimes as a squalid and inept sideplay to that arid Great Game of our times, the Cold War.

It is only since the last war that the economic buttressing of poor countries has been properly recognized as an instrument of State policy. Dollar imperialism is as old as Uncle Sam, but hitherto it has usually been based, frankly enough, upon the impulses of private self-advantage. In recent years it has dawned upon the political theorists that since poverty and frustration are the twin wombs of Communism, the best way to abort that awkward creed is to abolish poverty and frustration. This has led to some prodigal disbursements of public funds—money thrown helter-skelter down many an ill-flushed drain in the tired old belief that generosity will at least inspire gratitude, if not actually good government. It has also led to a contest of paternalism with the Soviet Union, a nation which has lately reached the same totally erroneous conclusions about the political consequences of generosity. Both sides are now learning that thanks are not votes, and that a really determined little State can accept good Communist cash with one hand and healthy capitalist dogma with the other. Among the recipients of aid from the United States, that prime old liberty man, are such uncompromising autocracies as Spain, Ghana, Persia, and Siam. Notable among the beneficiaries of Soviet aid is Egypt, a country whose fly-blown desert prisons shelter several hundred dedicated disciples of Marx. Several countries have discovered for themselves that the devil you don't know is far less attractive when you meet him horn to horn. In India, for instance, it came as a shock to many angry anti-imperialists to discover that the Russians who arrived to build them a steel mill displayed all the familiar aloofness of old-school sahibs: they, too, stockaded themselves in a little enclave of nostalgia, they too had snooty wives who spoke no foreign languages, they too unaccountably preferred vodka and borscht to vegetable curry and lemonade. The agents of progress are very alike, whatever their ideologies, and a Chinese engineer in Cuba can be just as bossy and insensitive as a Dutch commissioner in New Guinea.

Sometimes, too, this crass rivalry has to it elements of knockabout farce. The most theatrically symbolic arena of the struggle is Afghanistan, across whose prostrate but always twitching presence the Russians have, for more than a century, faced their opponents across the Asian divide. In the old days it was the British in India whose muzzle-loaders peered back across the Hindu Kush; today it is the Americans and their allies; but the flavor of the contest remains startlingly, almost ludicrously the same. Four times the British invaded Afghanistan, during the lifetime of the Raja, and it never did them the slightest good: the Americans and Russians have poured billions of dollars and rubles into the kingdom, without any detectable political effect. The Afghans are the slipperiest and wiriest of clients, and they long ago learned to play off one titan against the other, with results always profitable to themselves. The Russians have paved their capital city for them. The Americans have organized their airline. The Russians have built them a bakery. The Americans have given them a university. The Russians have thrown highways across their fierce interior. The Americans have built them an enormous airfield at Kandahar. The Russians are ensconced in one Ministry, the Americans in another. Wherever you go, you will meet the gleaming station wagons that represent one pulsing ideology or the swart high-axled jeeps that are emissaries of the other.

Any morning in the Ariana Hotel in Kabul you may see the Russian technicians preparing for the day's philanthrophy: five to a bedroom, portly, thick-set men who look as though they have never laughed in their lives except at obscure technical badinage, and who are to be seen through half-open doors wearing baggy brown pajamas, gargling out of chipped mugs, or scrubbing their chests with nailbrushes. Down the road, though, at that very same moment of the morning, the Americans are similarly preparing: their fin-tailed convertibles await them in the carport, their hygienic mouthwash stands ready-mixed, their vacuum-packed breakfast cereal crackles in the box, and Junior is already playing with his plastic moon terminal on the sprinkled lawn. Briskly they bolt their breakfasts, Riley and Ivanov both. Purposefully they step into their cars, with a Detroit purr or a Kiev rumble. Confidently they hasten away to their offices or building sites, sure in the knowledge that they are serving cause and country. They are like rival sugar-daddies courting the same wide-eyed blonde: and just as the blonde is often not half so dumb as she looks, so it sometimes crosses the Afghan mind, I suspect, that there's one born every minute.

This competitive benevolence is today's most powerful instrument for hastening the universal technical revolution, for transplanting in the poor world the mechanical civilization that Russians and Americans willy-nilly share. By far the greatest external sources of development funds are the American official agencies, and by far the greatest prod to western generosity is the possibility that the Russians may offer more. Sometimes it does no harm. Politically the Afghans are as independent as ever. Materially they can only benefit. The roads are paved. The bakery does bake. The university is probably excellent, and the airport at Kandahar certainly looks impressive (even if, being situated in possibly the most inconvenient position in Asia, not many aircraft seem to use it). Thoughtless and unselective aid, though, can lead peoples of less resilient character into bad habits. To put it at its most prosaic, it encourages loose practices of management and autocracy: if you can get one hundred million dollars out of a sugar-daddy, you can probably squeeze two. It leads nations to suppose that they can feed permanently upon the rivalry between the Powers. It sometimes keeps alive regimes that have no right to survive, which would in the natural course of political evolution soon topple into the limbo of discredited despotisms. Worst of all, it sustains the Cold War itself, makes its protagonists feel that they must always outbid each other, vulgarizes and degrades the very notion of generosity.

The Road to Huddersfield:

It should be axiomatic among the Powers that one of the duties of wealth is charity—a word that is still suspect among small States as among impoverished relatives but that best sums up the combined abstractions of love, hope, generosity, and good sense. As the Sanskrit proverb has it, "all we can hold in our two dead hands is what we have given away." The inequalities of the world are not merely dangerous or grotesque. They are terribly wrong, and as the citizen of the West reaches for his remote-control television selector, he would do well to remember that (to pluck a statistic almost at random) in Southeast Asia the infant mortality rate is four times as high as it is in western Europe, and life expectancy is less than half as long. To my mind, the living standards of the western world have reached a standard that is more than adequate and that, so long as there are still palsied beggars in the streets of Lima, or potbellied starving children in Indian railroad stations, is actually immoral. There are three proper justifications for the perpetual increase of wealth in the rich countries. The first is self-defense: the legitimate desire of a civilization to protect its own kind of society against the predacity of rivals. The second is continuity: the right of a people to provide for its children all the comforts and advantages it has enjoyed itself. But the third and most important is charity: the duty of a rich man to help his neighbor, of the strong to support the weak, of the sanguine to encourage the despondent. Many Englishmen have doubts about the union of their old kingdom with the continent of Europe, with all its possible corrosion of ancient traditions and staunch values; but morally they have little choice, for without the economic fillip such an association can bring them, they cannot play their part in helping the aspirant countries toward fulfillment—the principal duty of our age for Powers with a conscience. Many Americans regret their country's lavish programs of overseas aid, despairing of its frequent naïveté and incompetence, and scoffing at a policy that can pour good dollars into States of such desperate uncertainty as Laos or Bolivia. But posterity will say, I have no doubt, that for all its errors and false motives, the post-war American structure of foreign help, from the Marshall Plan to the Alliance for Progress, has been one of the nobler aberrations of history.

A flood of goodwill has, in fact, eddied during the past two decades from the rich world to the poor, from men of sophistication to men of simplicity. The various aid programs of the United Nations have not always been conspicuous for practical efficiency, but have always oozed benevolence. The youth movements in Britain and America which have sent young people out to work in the poor countries have attracted candidates of the highest caliber. All over the world individual reformers or visionaries are trying, in small pockets of initiative, to usher one small segment of humanity out of the past into the present. There is the fire-eating Danilo Dolci in Sicily, for example, with his home-made dams and his self-help classes. There is the Belgian mystic Father Pire, with his village reclamation schemes in East Pakistan. The crippled South African liberal Christopher Gell, whose blazing reformist energies sprang like fire from his iron lung in Port Elizabeth, was playing just such a part in the South African industrial revolution as Wilberforce and his friends did in the British—for often if you examine one of the fearful politi-

The Road to Huddersfield:

cal dilemmas of our day, you will find it to be, in deepest essence, only Huddersfield and the Luddites over again.

Most of the richest countries now have their overseas development institutes: the Russians even have a university specifically for the training of Africans and Asians. I can scarcely bear to remember the mountains of platitudes which have, at one recent time or another, been mouthed on the need for universal progress. I can scarcely enumerate the myriad benevolent societies which are always at work, hag-ridden by guilt or avid for salvation, raising the standard of Asian, African, or South American living. ("I swear this is my last luncheon," says an ample lady in a Lichty cartoon, helping herself to more trifle at the Benefit Luncheon for the Underfed Kuka-Burras. "These benefits to aid the undernourished and underprivileged nations are *ruining* my figure.") Desperate indeed have been the euphemisms coined to clothe the naked fact of backwardness: underprivileged, underdeveloped, less-developed, emergent, aspirant, nascent, blossoming, burgeoning. Prolix to a degree are the organizations of economic aid: the Colombo Plan, the International Finance Corporation, the Export-Import Bank, Point Four, the Special Fund, the International Monetary Fund, the Economic and Social Council, the International Co-operation Administration. There is to the very vocabulary of economic development something so thuddingly boring that intelligent men hastily close their books when they see an investment scheme in the next paragraph, and honest, earnest housewives find themselves dizzy with all the initials of international philanthropy and all the digits of enlightened self-interest.

Anyone surveying this tumult of assistance from a distance

and collating it as I am with the historical fact of Huddersfield will be impressed, I think, by its volume and variety but depressed by its flabby, ambivalent, and often amateurish lack of co-ordinated purpose. There is precious little international teamwork in boosting the progress of the poor world. The immense national programs of aid and investment are often tarnished by ulterior motives; most of them are "tied loans," which means that they must be used to buy the products of the lending State. Methods of lending or giving money are often slipshod, by professional banking standards, and sometimes suspect. Many good men are concerned with the problem, but so are many bad ones—duds, charlatans, men with an eye to an easy dollar, a decoration, or a safe pension, myriads of those perpetual wanderers through the international organizations of the world, UNRRA to UNICEF to WHO to UNESCO, who bring to the sphere of global philanthropy a suggestion of cultured but ineffectual dilettantism.

It all looks rather a mess, by the taut standards of the old industrialists. Money flows criss-cross in all directions, often wasted in projects of showy extravagance, often helping to keep an autocrat in furs and convertibles or a slippery contractor in business. Great things indeed are happening everywhere, from the splendid High Dam in Egypt to the huge hydroelectric schemes of the Andes, projects worthy of Pharaohs or Incas. There is scarcely a corner of the world that has not struck the first hammer blow, pulled the first steam cock of mechanization; but impelled as this great historical process is by an endless range of motives, from true-blue jingoism to sober economic necessity, the waste of time, effort, around the corner.

end is desirable, but few are prepared to co-operate in the means.

This book concerns one institution that approaches all the perennial Huddersfields in a spirit not always imaginative and not always inspired, but at least always professional. It is related by birth to the United Nations, but in effect it represents the economic energies of the capitalist West, and it flatters itself upon evading all those muzzy, fluttering, tangled imbroglios that ensnare most international activities. In size and in scope its efforts are relatively small, jottings in the margin of history, but in style it stands all on its own, for it advances to the help of the poor world with a gait that is calculating, steady, and a little overbearing, with frequent pauses for injunctions and second thoughts, and an air of hard-headed, unsentimental technical assurance. It sponsors no luncheons for the Underfed Kuka-Burras, though its intentions are, *au fond*, unimpeachably charitable. It is an attempt to funnel money from many different countries into a considered and balanced series of projects, and it is run on lines as strict, orthodox, and correct as any padded Wall Street banking house.

A few pedants still know this heavy paragon as the International Bank for Reconstruction and Development; but most people prefer to call it, with a sniff or a sneer, a riot or a genuflection, the World Bank.

2

*A funny place, origins and aims,
how it works,
the clearinghouse, Eugene Black,
criticisms, qualities,
dams, pipes, and newsprint,
"At least He's consistent"*

1

WASHINGTON, D.C., is full of funny places—funny peculiar, that is, not often funny ha-ha—but few are much funnier than 1818 H Street, where the World Bank lives. It is a big, new, faceless, rectangular building, of the sort that suddenly shrivels up your curiosity and leaves you positively anxious not to know what happens inside. In capitals of more dreadful temper, it might be the headquarters of the secret police, or the Ministry of National Correction, except for the sweet smiles the elevator girls give you. As it is, there is a frigid sense of the future to the building—that icy supranational future when wastrels will not be welcomed and prodigals not easily forgiven, when you will blush to boast yourself an Italian or a Finn, and delete from your very consciousness the words *"rule Britannia."* Down the street from the Bank there are two delightful second-hand bookshops, and there you may often see haggard financiers, looking slightly sheepish, stocking themselves up with Zane Grey or P. G. Wodehouse before returning, like astronauts after furlough, to the lunar hygiene around the corner.

The Road to Huddersfield:

There is nothing escapist about the World Bank. It was born in solemnity, and it works with a deliberate purpose to a well-defined and scrupulously honored set of rules. It was conceived at the Bretton Woods economic conference in 1944, when the financial bigwigs of the allied Powers, dominated by the influence of Roosevelt and the physical presence of Keynes, assembled to consider the economic consequences of yet another peace. They designed the bank as an institution that would mobilize sources of capital to help reconstruct the war-shattered countries and develop the backward ones. Its stockholders would be those nations that chose to join it—poor nations and rich ones, borrowers and lenders, subscribing capital and pledging credit according to their means. It was to stimulate afresh the international flow of money, dried up by the war, that had already begun the transformation of the poor regions. It was to act as a catalyst, a channel, a junction of monies—rather as the City of London had been the clearinghouse of nearly all foreign investment in the first decades of the century, and the great banking houses of Wall Street in the years between the wars—but at the same time it was to be a Bank of Governments and an associate of the United Nations: rather a vague kind of associate, which the Bank's own cautious lawyers like to describe as "a specialized agency within the meaning of Article 57 of the Charter." This was a conception so novel that nobody quite knew what to call the thing. "It was accidentally born with the name Bank," says one official memoir, "and Bank it remains, mainly because no satisfactory name could be found in the dictionary for this unprecedented institution." The banking community greeted the phenomenon with understandable skepticism, but Lord Keynes was undismayed. "How much better," said he in one of his more laborious aphorisms, "that our projects should begin in disillusion than that they should end in it."

The Bank got off to a muffled kind of start, but presently evolved an image all its own. Gradually the skeptics realized that there was to be nothing fuddy-duddy or starry-eyed about the World Bank. It was to be run on severe and uncompromising banking lines, and its purpose would be to make loans, like any other bank, to guarantee loans from other sources, and to stimulate private investors to put their money into worthy foreign ventures. Its purpose would be charity, in the widest sense, but charity of a strict and improving kind, the sort that a Victorian paterfamilias might dispense, with many an injunction of morality and many an improving text to a younger son setting up a steamcar factory of his own. The Bank was to be financed in the first place by its member governments, and thus the risks of defaulted debts would be shared in proportion among the nations. Of the subscriptions, only a small fixed percentage could be lent to borrowers, and all the rest would be held in reserve as a guarantee fund, enabling the Bank to prod private investors from a position of well-heeled strength. At the same time, the Bank would never guarantee more money than its own capital and reserves, making it in theory as stable an institution as the most nervous speculator could demand. The founding fathers were adamant that politics should be kept out of the institution, and later the Bank itself, with an eye to the abysmal record of international finance between the wars, became almost obsessed with the need to lend money sensibly and selectively. Before a penny passed the cashier's

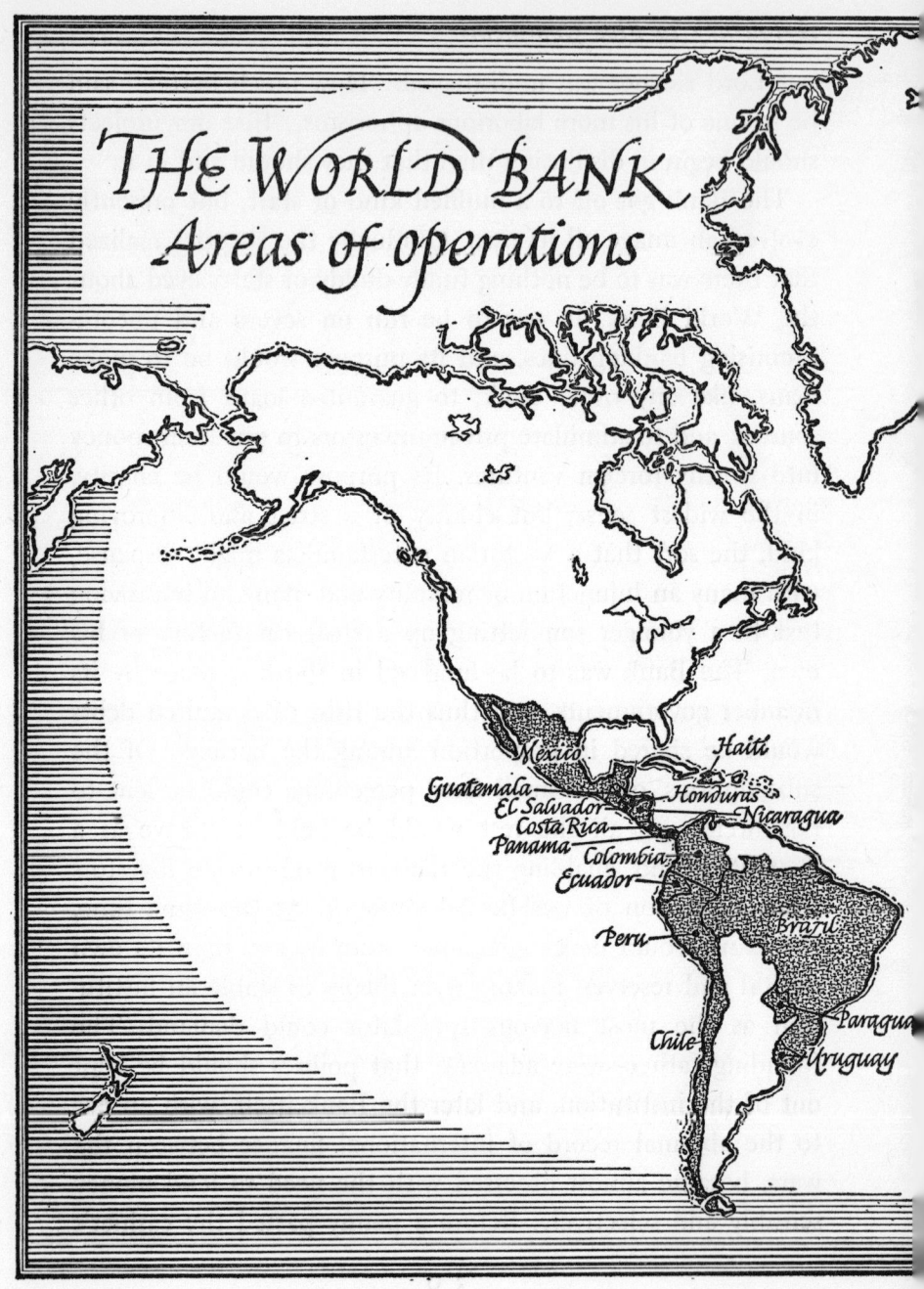

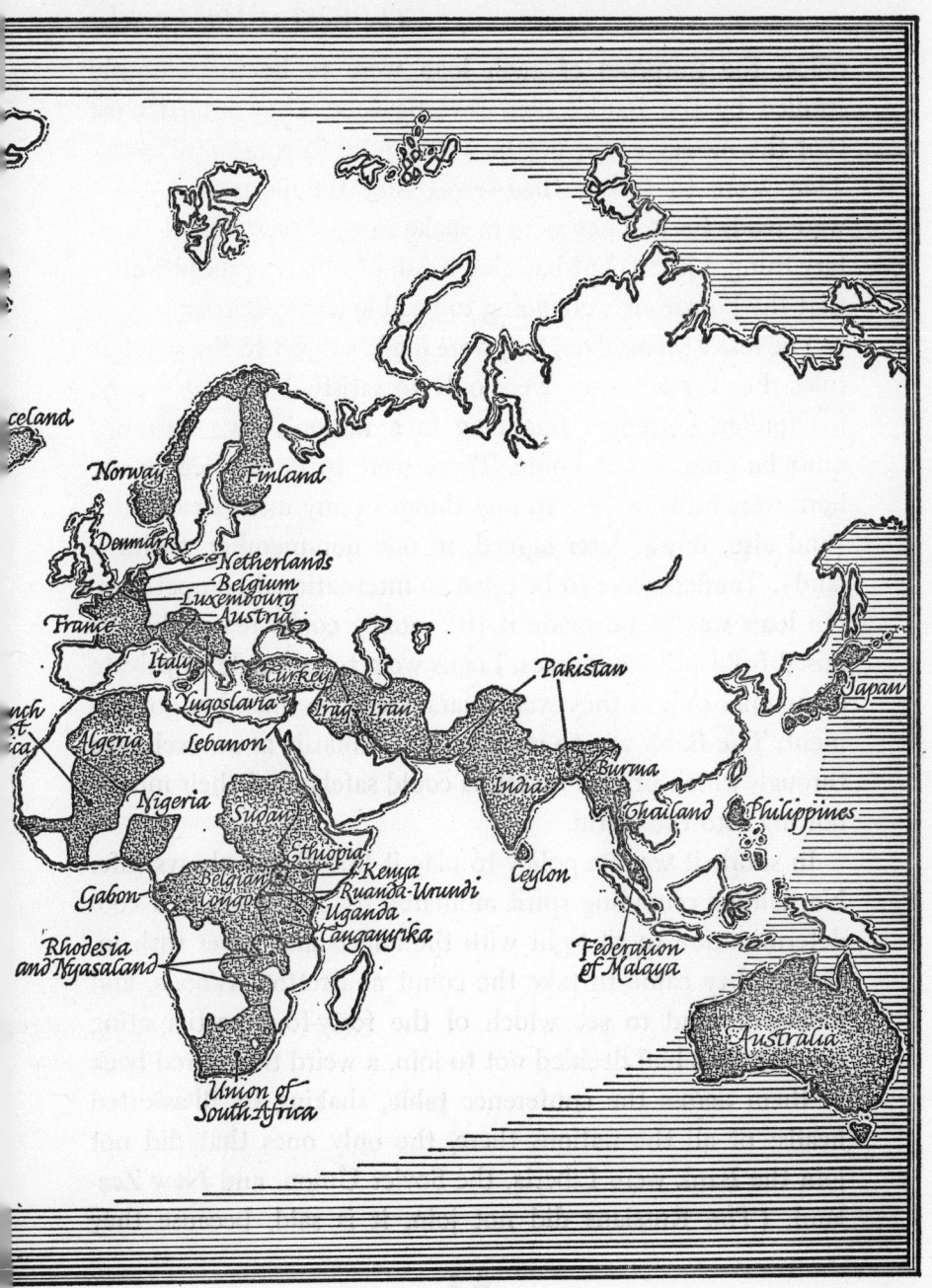

office, the purposes of each loan were to be meticulously studied by the Bank's own investigators. They were to see that the money could not be better used in some other way. They were to satisfy themselves that the borrowers really were ready for it. They were to make sure—it seems an elementary thing, I know, but banking is full of nursery precautions— that the borrowers were going to be able to pay it back.

The loans themselves, too, were made subject to the strictest rules. For a start, they were only to satisfy a country's need for foreign currency: financing in a nation's own currency must be obtained at home. There were to be no tied loans: borrowers must be free to buy things in any member country (and also, it was later agreed, in one non-member, Switzerland). Tenders were to be open to international competition. No loan was to be made if the money could reasonably be raised from private sources. Loans were to be made to private companies only if they were guaranteed by a member government. The Bank was to regard itself primarily as an exchange through which private investors could safely send their money flowing into the world.

In short, it was its policy to play it liberal but always safe. No flaming crusading spirit animated its origins—only a cool determination to sit tight with the angels and never rush in. When they came to take the count at Bretton Woods, and looked around to see which of the forty-four participating governments had decided not to join, a weird trio glared back at them across the conference table, shaking its ill-assorted heads: of all the nations there, the only ones that did not join the Bank were Liberia, the Soviet Union, and New Zealand. (The Russians did not join, it is said, because they would have had to reveal the size of their gold reserves; the Liberians and New Zealanders changed their minds just eighteen years later.)

This strange organism prospered, so satisfactorily that by 1962 there were seventy-five member States. The Bank soon abandoned its duties of reconstruction. The needs of a shattered Europe were far beyond its resources, and the rebuilding of the West was left, in effect, to the mammoth instrument of generosity called the Marshall Plan, which Churchill nominated the most unsordid act of history. The Bank presently devoted all its energies to development, and turned all its bankers' acumen to the world-wide technical revolution. It can hardly be denied that inextricably mixed up in its attitudes was a conviction that capitalism was the right way, that private enterprise was best, and, as a rule-of-thumb dogma, that the less State interference, the better. This was perhaps inherent to the composition of the thing: the United States put up nearly half the original capital. It became inescapable when Europe was split by the Iron Curtain, and both Poland and Czechoslovakia left the Bank. This was no crude bludgeon of the Cold War, distributing largesse as a politician hands out kisses, but it was frank enough in its sympathies. It was a bank, a proper bank, run by professional bankers, lending money at rates of interest not extortionate but scarcely open-handed, expecting to see a profit on its cash and on the projects it financed, raising its own funds largely by the selling of bonds on the open market. It was an instrument of applied capitalism. It was the skill, experience, and conviction of Wall Street and the City harnessed, con-

The Road to Huddersfield:

sciously but not without irony, to the accomplishment of a revolution.

I cannot say that 1818 H Street is exactly exciting, at least for an observer of my temperament. It badly needs a few more romantics, eccentrics, stage Irishmen, and cranks. It has, however, a powerhouse air to it, a hum and a hiss, as of some well-greased polished machine pumping or grinding or calculating to the smallest possible degree of precision with the least possible human attention. The World Bank is an unusually intricate mechanism, even as banks and powerhouses go, but after nearly two decades in gear, it seems to run exceedingly smoothly, without breakdown or demur (except when the miserable winter blizzards of Washington, sweeping out of the prairies, freeze up the capital and send the whole staff hang-dog home at lunchtime).

You have only to poke about the place for an hour or two, and look at the name cards on the doors, to realize how delicate and involved an organization this is. The constitution of the World Bank is subtle, and takes some understanding. Each member country nominates a governor, who is usually either the head of the State Bank at home or the Minister of Finance. When the governors assemble for their annual meeting, it is a gathering of the most powerful financial brains in the western world (two out of three meetings are held in Washington, but every third year they escape, with a whoopee and a rustle of ball gowns, to some more gilded capital). These grandees, though, are generally busy raising bank rates and making aldermanic speeches at home, and they are represented at H Street by eighteen full-time executive directors, who have their offices in the Bank building and also assemble three or four times a month in genial conclave.

Now, this is not so straightforward a system as it sounds, for the Bank is far from innocently democratic. The voting power of each director depends upon the money his country has put into the Bank: the United States now commands some 30% of the total vote, while the Republic of Panama can boast less than a quarter of 1%. What is more, by a complex and sometimes quixotic series of elective arrangements, the votes of the eighty-one members have been shared out, so to speak, among the eighteen executive directors. Five major stockholders nominate a director to represent themselves alone—the United States, France, Germany, Great Britain, and India. The other members elect thirteen directors to represent them all, and each director casts the votes of the countries that elected him. Thus the Australian director casts the votes of New Zealand, South Africa, and Vietnam too. The Pakistani represents not only the United Arab Republic but also Iran, Saudi Arabia, the Sudan, Iraq, Kuwait, Ethiopia, Jordan, Lebanon, and the Syrian Arab Republic. The Belgian represents Korea, the Moroccan Malaya, the Dutch director both Israel and Yugoslavia. One man speaks for Mexico, Peru, Venezuela, Guatemala, El Salvador, Honduras, Haiti, Nicaragua, Costa Rica, and Panama, but, even so, his total voting power is only a tenth of the United States delegate's. So realistic but oddly topsy-turvy are these arrangements that when Cuba crossly left the Bank in 1961, her executive director remained in his office at H Street (he had, after all, nine other clients to think of).

You might suppose that these strange groupings would

The Road to Huddersfield:

often lead to awkward disputes, and indeed, as you walk past the executive directors' offices and hear the discordant babble of voices within, the gutturals and the sibilants, clipped and florid in antiphony, it is difficult to see how the Bank can conduct its affairs any less petulantly than its fractious relative on the East River. In practice, however, all seems to go peacefully. This is partly because each director must cast *all* his votes one way: when the Board unanimously approved a loan to Egypt for the improvement of the Suez Canal, it did not mean that the Israeli government approved the project, only that (presumably) the Dutch and the Yugoslavs did. It is partly because every issue is thoroughly hammered out between the Bank's management and the executive directors before it comes formally before the Board: if one or two of the big stockholders objected strongly enough, a project would probably be dropped, anyway. But it is mostly because the World Bank is a technocracy. At 1818 H Street, what the management says goes. The Board usually accepts its judgment, and has never rejected a formal proposal by the management in all the history of the institution.

The staff of the World Bank is international, though it leans heavily in the direction of what old-school Europeans like to call the Anglo-Saxon. The President is American, one of the Vice-Presidents is British, the Secretary is Canadian, the Director of Technical Operations is Dutch. At least fifty nationalities are represented, but many critics would like to see more Frenchmen there, and many realists think there should be more Germans. Many of its staff members, who are nearly all men, are boring to a degree. Many others are unexpectedly lively (one of the liveliest of them all defied me to write an interesting book about the Bank, and another keeps Nubian goats). All are extremely professional, and one department head has told me that if ever an applicant for a job gives as his reason the urge of philanthropy, he dismisses him at once.

These are do-gooders, but do not like to admit it. They may be excited by the unfolding of history all around them, but do not often let it show. They pride themselves upon their starkly businesslike approach to the needs of the poor nations, and would think it effete or namby-pamby to allow any breath of sentiment to creep between the ledger lines. They are usually paid about the same as United States civil servants, though their income is tax-free. The nature of the Bank's work, its immense range and ever-changing application, has drawn to H Street some men of liberal and original views, not the kind you normally expect to find disputing accounting practices or arguing theories of economic expansion.

There is an agreeable streak of astringency to the World Bank, to be encountered now and then in the plush staff restaurant on the twelfth floor or glimpsed refreshingly in the flicker of a caustic smile. There is a parallel element of gossip and clique: the Bank sometimes reminds me of an English cavalry mess soon after the arrival of a new colonel, when the officers break up in huddled murmuring groups, drinking port and saying nasty things about each other. Some of these men have been investment bankers all their lives. Some are economists. Some are engineers. Some have literary pretensions, and love to dispute a split infinitive or a purple passage. Many have slipped in by side doors—journalism, law, scholarship, government service, influential parentage, or beguiling man-

The Road to Huddersfield:

ners. Nearly all have now grown a little indistinct by the internationalism of their calling, and have come out rather pallid or air-conditioned, denuded of national warts or horny regional prejudices. There seem to be no national rivalries at H Street, no bickering loyalties or subterfuges of patriotism. Even La Gloire is silenced.

The ambience of the place, though, is all American: the smooth, swift, silent elevators, the elegant scented secretaries, the security guards in their blue uniforms (who wear the magic word "Burns" upon their caps, not from any poetic enthusiasm, but because a different Mr. Burns founded the company that provides them). "Develop a pleasing telephone manner!" says one of the Bank's pamphlets of secretarial advice. "Make the person who talks to you over the telephone glad he called you, by expressing in your tone of voice a real desire to be of assistance." A dreadful jargon clogs and congests the conversations of the Bank, deadened with truisms and bathos. "The first stage in launching a project," runs an observation I find recorded in my notebook, "is to choose an area in which to operate." "There is no prohibition," a Bank lawyer observed one day, explaining a point of policy, "against excluding non-members"—a sort of quintuple negative. "Overall completion of the entire plan," I once read in a progress report, "is estimated at approximately 75%"—which means that it was three-quarters finished. Bank people love to talk about positive-income elasticity of demand, about developmental situations in which utilization of resources has not reached an optimum, about projects being organizationally related to infrastructure investment, about end-use visits and debt-equity ratios and pay-out analyses and acquaintance missions and credit-worthiness. The language of economics is seldom limpid, but in H Street they usually manage to remove from it the very last flickering colophon of charm.

The Bank is a singularly self-contained affair. It has its own travel office, entrenched in airline pamphlets and flight bags, which maintains the largest of all accounts with American Express. It has its own translation bureau. It has its own dispensary, highly knowledgeable about dysenteries and vaccinations. It has a cafeteria of futuristic efficiency, entirely automative, where you may buy yourself an Infra-Reddy Hot Sandwich by slipping a dime in a slot. It has a records section of voluminous variety, and an information department of literate and shiny prolificity. It has a startling finance department, where they will show you blank checks payable at the State Banks of all eighty-one members (though the hard cash is banked elsewhere, with the Federal Reserve Bank of New York: the safe apparently contains nothing more tempting than the assets of the Stamp Club, and a burglar who once hopefully raided the place found only a driblet of assorted kyats, sucres, quetzals, and bahts, currencies which were probably as baffling to him as they are, if I may be so presumptuous, to you). An air of polished accomplishment informs the headquarters of the World Bank, and if you sometimes feel like dancing a crooked jig along its corridors, or chalking anti-nuclear slogans on its library wall, well, you can hardly demand frivolity within the meaning of Article 57.

This building is, above all, as its founders intended, a clearinghouse. The Bank itself is a mighty borrower. It was required by its original charter to finance projects that private investors would consider too risky; but, paradoxically, it was also required to raise most of its lending money from private investors. It was never intended that the subscriptions of the member nations would finance all the Bank's activities, and in fact only about two fifths of its loans have come out of its own capital. Nearly all the rest of the money has been raised by selling World Bank bonds on the public market.

This has not always been easy. Today the World Bank seems as solid an institution as any on earth. In 1946, when it began work, its reputation was much less reassuring. It was the oddest of unknown quantities, emanating a whiff of insubstantial international idealism, and surrounded by all those suggestions of whimsy and unorthodoxy that experienced investors most distrust. Nobody knew if it could be sued, for one thing. Nobody cared to forget the abysmal record of international investment before the war. Nobody trusted the novelties of its constitution. What is more, in many of the American States it was actually illegal for institutions like banks and insurance companies to buy international bonds— a relic of America's stiff-necked and suspicious isolationist past.

All this demanded skillful salesmanship and lobbying, and it has made 1818 H Street a formidable center of broking knowledge. As late as 1950 a flotation by the Bank was a sorry failure, but today its bonds are scarcely less in demand than those of the most glittering private corporations. You or I could buy them, if we had a mind. They have been sold to the public in Belgium, Canada, Germany, Great Britain, Holland, Italy, Switzerland, and the United States, just as governments often raise money by selling State bonds, or cities hopefully offer their own municipal issues. As a borrower the Bank has been an unpredicted success, and it has also managed to sell off many of its borrowers' obligations—which means that other people take over its loans in return for the substantial interest they earn. It has also, time and again, persuaded private investors to put money into foreign countries—chiefly by force of example and confidence—so that a World Bank loan has often released, as was specifically hoped at Bretton Woods, a flow of ordinary private funds. Nowadays the Bank is nothing if not respectable, and the very fact that it considers a State ripe for a loan is a kind of gilt-edge testimonial.

For it is not at all easy to squeeze money out of this Bank, and 1818 H Street is a clearinghouse, too, of carefully sorted information. Long and sticky are the inquiries that are made before a cent is handed out. First the Wulustan government must send its own representative to Washington to explain the project it wants the hundred billion dollars for and convince the Bank that the Wulustan Textile, Mineral, and General Development Corporation, Inc., really knows the difference between long staple and taconite. The Bank, in return, then sends a mission to Wulustan to sniff out the general economic condition of that hopeful federation, and to see whether WTMGDC ought really to have priority or whether money could better be spent in other ways. The government may be asked to provide a lot more facts; or a second mission may be sent; or the Wulustan embassy in Washington may be consulted; or there may be a protracted and detailed exchange of correspondence (the Bank has no diplomatic bag, but sends a pouch of mail regularly to its European office in

The Road to Huddersfield:

Paris). If all goes well, a team of negotiators from Wulu City goes to Washington, and a draft agreement is hammered out. The executive directors, who have been kept informed all along, almost certainly approve this at their next Board meeting, and presently the contract is signed to the flash of a staff photographer's bulb and a rasp of bankers' bonhomie. (The money goes out by cable or mail. It is nearly always repaid by cable, because if it were mailed, interest would be chargeable on the days consumed in the post: it has never occurred to any of the eighty-one State Banks, so far as I can make out, to mail the check a little earlier.)

The Uruguayans took ten years to work out one of their loans. It took four and a half years to write and adopt Brazilian legislation demanded by the Bank as a prerequisite for agreement. On the other hand, the Australians raised a loan of $100 million in twenty-two days flat. The Bank inspects its several customers with a cool and analytical eye. A constant stream of information, like the dispatches of our intelligence network, arrives from its Paris office and from its representatives living, for one period or another, in Nicaragua or Siam, Panama or Haiti, Peru or Pakistan. There are the reports to be studied in the 1,800 newspapers, magazines, and bulletins that arrive regularly at H Street. There are the reports compiled on the progress of each separate project: the Bank keeps its sharp eye on all the work until the last stone is laid and the last dollar repaid. There are the reports of innumerable technical teams always at work somewhere or other: when I checked the lists at random one day I found that eighteen people, about one in twenty of the professional staff, were at that moment traveling somewhere in the world—in Chile,

Mexico, Ireland, Malaya, Japan, Lebanon, West Germany, Switzerland, and Ghana. There are the reports of the working parties always studying specific projects, and the specialists who spend their whole lives in the contemplation of a particular State. There are, perhaps turgid but most telling of all, the enormous reports of the general survey missions, groups of eminent experts who examine a country's complete economic condition as thoroughly as any consort of specialists dissects a millionaire's physique. They are no mere tabulated pamphlets that these savants produce, but books of a most ample girth. *The Basis of a Development Program for Colombia*, for example, which a Bank mission produced in 1950, is more than 600 pages long, and includes among its sections one on Financial Aspects of Capital Formation, one on railroad administration, one on the condition of rural housing, one on the prevalence of intestinal infection, one on air cargo rates, one on the telephone service, one on the export of bananas, and one—the best of the lot—on *smuggling*. The Bank has produced such analyses of more than a score of countries; though not one of them, alas, has ever implemented all a mission's proposals, and the Cubans, once invited to consult A *Development Program for Cuba*, couldn't even find their copy.

There is a great deal of technical knowledge in the Bank, contributed by engineers who have worked in all climates and latitudes of the earth, and who bring to the institution an element of detached and horny realism that often wings a high-flown theory or punctures a pretension from the start. There is a daunting volume of theoretical economic knowledge: the Bank supports its own Economic Development

The Road to Huddersfield:

Institute, a sort of staff college for officials from the poor countries, and also runs a less exalted training scheme for junior visiting bigwigs (it was there, I think, that I once found a group of haggard young unfortunates discussing "A Symposium on Simultaneous Equation Estimation, by Ta-Chung Liu and L. R. Klein"). There is much esoteric legal knowledge: a whole new body of international law has been built up, year after year, by the operations of this unprecedented organism. All in all, stored away in the coffers of the Bank there now lies an accumulation of information about most of the poor countries of the earth which many a foreign office would covet and many an earnest newspaper give its masthead for.

Even so, there are gaps in the expertise. The world is split grandly into five departments at H Street, but this majestic division, like the Papal Partition of the New World, is self-deceptive. The Bank's officials, closeted as they usually are with government spokesmen and economic apologists, are sometimes naïvely out of touch with the true temper of a country: and a few of them seem specifically designed by a mischievous creator to have wool pulled over their eyes.

During my first week or two at the World Bank it seemed to me that something was missing. I was not grasping the core of the place, the spindle around which its activities revolved, and it felt rather like watching a lively game of football in which the players were unprovided with a ball. Later I came to realize that this was a political phenomenon, for the Bank is a sort of autocracy, and everything in that enormous building circles around, leads up to, or frequently runs away from the President. The head of the World Bank has far more power and latitude than his opposite number in any private banking corporation. He is not only the head of the management but chairman of the Board, too, and his word, for all the distinguished lieutenants fluttering around him, is unquestionably law. Since 1949 the office has been held continuously by one man—through three American presidencies, two British reigns, a couple of French republics, a Stalin and a Khrushchev, a Farouk and a Nasser, a Korea, a Suez, a Hungary, and a Cuba. This overwhelming accretion of experience and authority has vastly increased the stature of the job, and made the President of the World Bank not only a despot in his own office but a man of great power and influence in the world at large.

Eugene Black, who held this portentous office for so many years, retired in 1963, but the Bank is still molded largely in his image, and even now his presence there is inescapable: for many a long year yet any book about this institution will be a book about him. He is a rangy, handsome Southerner, whose grandfather, Henry Grady, was a famous spokesman of the South, and who retains in his slow and rather stylized courtesy much of the fabled Dixie charm. He has been a financier all his life, one of the most persuasive of American investment bankers, but he has an ambassadorial air to him, and a wider range of interests than most contemporary bankers. (Though as a matter of fact it was a vice-president of J. P. Morgan's who recently wrote the standard work on Mushrooms in Russian History, as part of an encyclopedic study of that fungus. I once told him that I had recently visited a Nepalese river valley called the Khumbu. A wild gleam lit his eye as I pro-

The Road to Huddersfield:

nounced the name, for it was, I think he told me, the Sanskrit for "toadstool.")

It used to be an agreeable but somehow tantalizing experience to visit Black in his rooms high in H Street, with their spectacular views over Washington and the Potomac. Perhaps he was washing his hands when you arrived, and you would hear him whistling in the adjoining bathroom (at least I swear I sometimes heard him, though he is said to be tone-deaf and incapable of whistling at all). You might then inspect the bric-a-bric that festooned his spacious office, and try to reach some pre-conclusion about his character. Here was a picture of the high-funneled American destroyer in which he served during World War I. Here was a scroll of honor in Spanish, presented to him by the Government of Ecuador. Here was a golden Japanese helmet. Here was a bust of a Polish miner carved in coal, a forlorn relic of the days when the poor Poles were members of this institution. Here was a photograph of a performance of *Hamlet* staged by Africans in Southern Rhodesia; they wore togas, and looked triumphantly actor-managerial. There were golfing pictures galore, and galleries of celebrated contemporaries, and marvelous maps, and innumerable certificates of honorary degrees, and a few gently disrespectful cartoons of the President himself.

The display was likely to leave you intrigued but unenlightened; and when into this luxurious and intensely personal milieu Black presently strode, rubbing his hands together and slightly smiling, you would find yourself no less confused, I suspect, by his enigmatic quality. He is a tall man, balding, rather stooped, with an amused and ironic face and an elegant languor of motion, and he leaves you always guessing. Is he a great man or only an accomplished bond salesman? Is he more clever than he seems or stupider? Is he nice or nasty, leader or led, frank or less than candid, chess master or poker king? I confess I have never made up my mind, but I do know that he is a man of memorable presence, the kind of figure of whom our descendants will say, a century from now, that they remember him well, as clear as daylight: he had a long white beard, like Napoleon.

Black has long cherished an insatiable passion for Shakespeare, and this is a key to one aspect of his character. He projects, for all his elegance and cultivation, a slight and pleasant suggestion of the homespun, as so many Shakespearean addicts do. I do not mean that he approaches the plays with any naïveté. He knows them intimately, possesses most of them in the great Variorum edition, and is a familiar habitué of the Shakespearean scholarly societies. (In 1959 he devoted his summer holiday to a Birmingham University symposium at Stratford, and snide critics like to say that for fourteen years the affairs of the International Bank for Reconstruction and Development were really governed from Anne Hathaway's cottage.)

There is, though, to the very avidity and thoroughness of this interest, something unexpectedly unsophisticated (I would almost venture to say, were it not for the sniggers I can already hear, innocent). Black loves those plays, and once told me that he would like to spend the rest of his life elucidating some neglected facet of Shakespearean scholarship—inflationary spirals in Bohemia, perhaps, or debt-equity ratios in the Forest of Arden. This detached and apparently guileless enthusiasm reflects what seems to me his greatest asset: his

The Road to Huddersfield:

gift of apparent simplicity. He has the knack of easy exposition. He never talks in the oppressive jargon of his trade. He never uses unnecessarily technical words, or even unnecessarily long ones. He has a talent for the direct approach and the straight answer, for reducing immensely complicated subjects into terms of ordinary relevance. He occasionally suggests to me some imperturbable old-school general (Confederate, of course), statuesque amid the grapeshot, summing up some frantic and crucial crisis in four or five words of horsey slang. There is nothing patronizing about him, nothing condescending, and no earnest academic or lick-spittle progressive could have been more successful in dealing with touchy emissaries from Afro-Asia. "I don't much like your Bank," an Indian delegate is once said to have told them at H Street, "but that Black—he's a charmer!"

With clarity goes flexibility. Black is not at all a rigid or dogmatic man, nor is he stuck in any proper channels. His mind is tempered, of course, by a lifetime of American finance, so that you would hardly expect him to suddenly embrace the principles of State socialism, for example, or sponsor some new movement of extreme economic heresy. He likes new ideas, nevertheless, and pragmatic approaches, and unexpected slants, and unheralded gleams. He enjoys both Balzac and baseball, and has read the whole of Conrad's works. He was perfectly prepared to commission a book about his Bank from a writer without the slightest knowledge of, and only a vestigial interest in, banking. He always had very firm ideas about the purposes of his institution, but he never demanded uniformity —in men, in methods, even in principles. He is a Southern gentleman, and an American financier too, yet he has a genuine sympathy for the internationalist trend of the times. He would agree, I think, that patriotism is not enough. He liked being President of the World Bank because the job transcended the more prosaic boundaries of personal profit and national prestige. I once asked him whom, of all the statesmen of his acquaintance, he most admired, and his choice was Nehru. He got on well with President Nasser. He established, during his term of office, a meshwork of contacts—what the English call "the old boy net"—with distinguished financiers in most countries of the West, through which many a gigantic project was first mooted and many a rash approach rebuffed from the start.

Black's stature, so everyone agrees, enormously increased during his tenure of the presidency, and during his last years at H Street he really did feel, as Hammarskjoeld did, a man whose loyalties go beyond flag-wavings and parochial slogans. After the war, I am told, the State Department was not beyond bringing pressure to bear on the Bank, in pursuance of some national or ideological ambition. (The first President, Eugene Meyer, actually resigned because of American interference in the running of the place.) By the 1960's, although the United States still commanded a third of both votes and capital, no Secretary of State, I think, would have dared to bring improper influence to bear upon Eugene Black.

Still, many people dislike this man. It was always easy enough, as you sat there on the other side of his immense polished desk, to imagine some of his faults. He is a vain man, like most of us. He has, I would hazard to guess, a more limited intellectual range than his sycophants would allow: others wrote his speeches for him, and often conceived, I suspect, the lofty generalizations that helped to win him honorary degrees. You may think him a calculating man, almost secretive, and he can be unkind to fools. I am told that senior members of his staff found him always ready to listen, but younger men were sometimes insensitively rebuffed. He never seemed to resent, or even perhaps to notice, the sycophancy that attended him at H Street—the Shakespeare volume ostentatiously on a subordinate's desk, the sickly deference, the comical esteem. *Sing Me a Murder*, by Helen Nielsen, *Don't Forget to Write*, by Art Buchwald, and *Innocents at Home*, by Lord Kinross, were all on the Recommended Reading List when I once called on the Bank's staff library, but carefully heading the list was Eugene Black's *Diplomacy of Economic Development*. He is a poor administrator, with no eye for tedious detail and a tendency to get bored. He is a hypochondriac, and a practical joker, too. He speaks no foreign language, and he is susceptible, I think, to flattery.

But transcending all is his sense of style. Whatever he does is big. It was a fine thing to see Eugene Black swiveling in his chair before the vast map of the world that covered one wall of his room, bold with the symbols of his Bank's activities—a power plant in Peru, a dam in Siam, a canal in Pakistan, a nuclear reactor in Italy. He has a noble feeling for scale and scope, gracefully illuminated by a sense of fun that does not always turn into horse-play. A Danish scientist once called upon him with an idea for making cotton-seed husks into flour, which could, he said, not only be cooked into palatable foods, but would also, by nature of the cotton seed's properties, effectively reduce the reproductive capacity of males, thus helping to solve the population problem. Black instantly summoned the restaurant manager, gave him a sack of the stuff, and fed the entire board of executive directors with birth-control pancakes that very noon. Black's point of view is always strong and often idiosyncratic, whether it is his notorious lack of sympathy for Latin volatility or his inflexible refusal to read a book with the dust jacket on. He is a powerful, disturbing, possibly rather lovable man, and for a decade or more the Bank depended upon him like an army upon its marshal. As he roamed the world, his aides and advisers obsequiously swarmed about him, like thoughtful clanking staff officers with their maps and polished swords, or possibly lieutenants to some unusually urbane Al Capone. He was, in his time, by far the most interesting employee of the World Bank, and much the biggest. He ran the show. He set the style. Though he no longer sits up there in H Street, with the world on the wall behind him and his lieutenants attentive at his elbow, though you will no longer hear him whistling in the bathroom, it is Black's bank still.

He is one of the four or five people in history to have been awarded honorary degrees by Harvard, Yale, and Princeton all in the same week—one on a Monday, one on a Tuesday, one on a Thursday—and, more than any other man alive today, he is responsible for the distribution of the Huddersfield civilization among the simpler peoples of the earth.

"I do not much like your Bank." The World Bank has many critics, in all the continents, who are chiefly affronted by its tendencies toward the stuffy and the patronizing. Sometimes they express only the sort of ill-defined resentment a schoolboy feels against a severe headmaster—the inflamed

The Road to Huddersfield:

touchiness of the new nations so recently emancipated from sixth-form discipline and now enjoying the heady fervor of campus liberty. Sometimes they are stung by tactlessness or contempt: "The French learn a lesson," was the headline of one article about the Bank which described with waspish relish H Street's insistence that a loan to France "be used for industry, not night clubs." Others again reflect the suspicion that the Bank is not really a bank at all but an institution of political skulduggery, an extension of dollar diplomacy or a hidden fuse in the Cold War. And finally there are the reasoned strictures of economists, who sometimes feel that the Bank is too blinkered and demanding in its approaches to the poor countries, and bases its policies too rigidly upon the criteria of orthodox banking.

Few observers would deny that an unhappy air of superiority often issues from the place. I have sensed it all too strongly myself, from staff members who have been kind enough to read this manuscript and left me feeling as though I have just failed the entrance examination to a course of creative writing. It is amusing to see what diverse responses this sparks. I once attended the signing ceremony of a loan to some small member nation of the Bank—I forget which—for some not very grandiose project—I forget exactly what: lofty indeed was the condescension with which the Bank, whose purpose is the making of loans, agreed to make this one, and fawning to a degree was the deference with which the money was accepted, the borrowers' representative assuring the management that he was positively grateful for the difficulties the Bank had placed in their way, which had made them feel not only richer, but happier and more civilized too, and had convinced them, he seemed to suggest, that such obstructive and delaying tactics ought properly to be applied to the governing of all human affairs. On the other hand, an Indian delegate, once reminded fulsomely that the Bank had lent his country a total of $600 million, turned with a sweet but abrasive smile upon the management and offered them his hearty congratulations.

Repeatedly, in wildly disparate corners of the earth, bankers and engineers have complained to me, less bitterly than wryly, about the pedagogic attitudes of Bank representatives—often technicians, they say, with qualifications far inferior to their own. In South America particularly, where educated men by and large believe themselves to have inherited the European qualities in a particularly pure and elevated kind, beneficiaries of the World Bank seem to resent the hoity-toity airs of the hearty Americans, frigid British, or pallid Scandinavians who visit them: and one African assured me that it would take another half-century or more for the World Bank to understand how to properly address an Ethiopian gentleman. The World Bank does sometimes seem a little too self-satisfied, a little too portly for its functions, and there are intelligent men in 1818 H Street itself who believe that a staff restaurant of rather less opulent decor might have fed the brutes just as well.

More specifically, the Bank is often attacked for behaving too much like a profit-making organization and too little like an international body of essentially charitable purpose. The Bank indeed makes a substantial profit—it now has reserves roughly equal to the amount of its annual loans—and there are many economists who think it could afford to be more generous. Such critics complain that the Bank's experts expect too much of the new African and Asian administrations, set their sights too high and their standards too rigid. They believe the Bank's assessments are sometimes too elaborate, so that expensive foreign equipment is bought with its loans when second-hand tractors or bulldozers would do—or, better still, manual labor. They think the Bank is sometimes pig-headed in its principles: in particular, in its unyielding opposition to the use of inflation as an economic instrument (because inflation makes prices go up, it often attracts to a country, as it has to Brazil, foreign investors who see in it a prospect of quick and sometimes dazzling profit).

The tone of the Bank is often ponderously dogmatic. "It happens not infrequently," says one of its official publications, "that the Bank's examination of general economic conditions in the borrowing country reveals the existence of economic or financial practices or policies which so adversely affect the financial and monetary stability of the country that, if continued, they would endanger both the productive purposes and the repayment prospects of a Bank loan. In such cases, it is the policy of the Bank to require, as a condition of Bank financing, that the borrowing country institute measures designed to restore stability to its economy." Such an inflection of voice, such an assumption of unassailable superior knowledge, has understandably made enemies for the World Bank, and kept its critics always simmering.

Many Indians were furious when Black himself once suggested that New Delhi was relying too heavily upon State enterprise and not enough upon the good old capitalist system. The South Americans have often balked at the Bank's insistence that even State-owned electric-power companies should charge high enough rates to be self-supporting. The Lebanese were once disgruntled because they wanted to use a Bank loan to buy equipment from behind the Iron Curtain, a proposition which H Street huffily, if predictably, vetoed (though in fact there is nothing in the Bank's charter to forbid it—like the man said, it is only that there is no prohibition against the exclusion of non-members). North American manufacturers resent the alternative it offers to tied loans from the American government, which of course guarantee orders for American factories. Brazilians dislike the Bank almost as a matter of principle; and the Turks once expelled its representative from their territories.

It is often said that the Bank, in its determination to make sure that a project is sensible and profitable before it advances a cent, sometimes squashes an idea altogether—for it is the instant advance of money that would make it feasible. It is criticized for its reluctance to infuse money into a State's economy without specifying projects; for its refusal to finance the building of schools, the very basis of a technical society; for its tendency to favor nations that are semi-developed already; for its distrust of State development banks, its neglect of agriculture, its disregard of housing problems; for being, in sum, too hidebound, complacent, schoolmarmish, and straight-laced. The feeling is well expressed in a German cartoon that hangs endearingly in the Bank's information office. There stands this great organization as half the world, in its testier moments, envisages it: a tall, tight, beak-nosed old maid in pince-nez, pinched with stinginess, with a high lace fichu, two hatpins in her dowdy hat, and an expression on her

The Road to Huddersfield:

face that proclaims her principal pleasure in life to be the mortification of high-spirited small boys.

Much of this criticism is unquestionably true, but much of it is peripheral, if not actually irrelevant. The point is that the World Bank tries to do a fundamentally charitable job in an unmistakably businesslike way—partly because its own instincts are hard-headed and precise; partly because it has had to convince the business community at large of its own probity and efficiency. One might argue that another kind of institution altogether would help the poor peoples better: and this proposition, as we shall later see, the Bank partly accepts. The Bank lives, however, by being the kind of institution it is, and to nag it into compromise would be like pushing it halfway out of a penthouse window.

The severest critics of its manner will usually admit, under pressure, to some grudging admiration of its principles: maddening though I found those superior critics of my manuscript, I have to admit that they were often right. As Black says, the Bank is governed by two overriding and unimpeachable rules: it wants its money used well, and it wants to be paid back. The best thing about this institution is its absolute fairness. It has acquired to the world at large an aura of mysterious financial power, so that a hubbub of speculation used to pursue Eugene Black on his frequent journeys around the world. I do not believe, though, that there are many secret undercurrents swirling beneath its affairs, just as I regretfully confess myself unable to unearth any sizzling inside story of its activities, any juicy revelations or scandalous venalities. It is, for the most part, what it seems to be. It has a very clear conception of its functions and its limitations, and it treats all comers precisely the same, much as a duke might treat with equal condescension the village pharmacist and the Harley Street brain surgeon.

The World Bank's loans are certainly not cheap, but its interest rates are the same for all borrowers, and are directly related to the rate at which the Bank is itself borrowing money at the same time; in the past they have varied from 4% to 6¼%. If it does not make as many loans as it could, that is because it does not find, by its own scrupulous standards, enough suitable projects to finance: nobody can really accuse it of any shady commercial partialities. When a loan was made to the Filipinos for a power project, the money was spent, not only in the United States, as the skeptics might suppose, but also in West Germany, Finland, Japan, Britain, Italy, France, and Sweden. Sometimes the Bank does indeed sound patronizing as it hands over the cash, but its manner of spinster reluctance is sometimes inspired, I am assured, by the desire of many Wulustanis to brag of their accomplishment to the electorate at home: the harder it seems to be to squeeze money out of H Street, the better the boast will sound. Sometimes the sycophancy of the client States may well be false; but often they really are grateful for the rigid standards of the Bank, its incentives to think twice and sign later, to take a quick look at least, with one eye anyway, if possible with glasses on, before actually leaping. Visitors from the aspirant countries seem to leave H Street slightly exasperated by the flavor of it all but impressed all the same, and certainly the institution is never contemplated with that air of wry disillusionment with which people everywhere tend to regard the United Nations proper.

Politically it has mellowed and matured, and grown out of its callower Wall Street attitudes. It has made loans both to Nationalist China and to Communist Yugoslavia, and time and again it has publicly recognized the need for land and social reform in the ramrod backward States. It certainly would not welcome the admission of the Soviet Union and her allies, if only because their conception of money and its uses seems to be totally different from its own, and their presence might wreck the carefully balanced structure of the Bank's management: but I am told that Black himself was extremely indignant when one executive director suggested the delaying of Nigeria's admission until her future political leanings became clearer. Among professional financiers the Bank's reputation is, considering its equivocal status, astonishingly high. Among newspaper pundits, it has acquired a dim but lofty mystique, something between that of a very superior pawnbroker and that of a very effective secret service. Among the borrowing nations, it has established its authority so absolutely that not one loan has ever been defaulted: even at the bloodiest climax of the Congo imbroglio, payments due to the Bank emerged as regular as clockwork out of the chaos.

The part it plays in the world technical revolution is marginal, or perhaps lubricant. It was seen from the start, not as a prime mover, but as a conduit or catalyst. The sums it deals in, though prodigious to the lay mind, are small compared with the astronomical outlays of the various American agencies, or even set beside the volume of private investment that flows from the rich countries to some of the poor. But a World

Bank loan is a sort of guarantee of a nation's probity, and it is also a chit to say that the borrower can now use money properly, is reaching the requisite level of technique and stability. Often valuable private investment has directly followed a Bank loan; sometimes the Bank has arranged that a loan shall actually coincide with a public raising of funds, by the same borrower, on the investment market—rather as a man who has just come into a small fortune might simultaneously take out a Diners' Club card. What is more, as we shall presently discover, the well-heeled but still brass-tack character of the Bank has qualified it more than once as an international mediator: for even over a diplomatic conference table, nothing talks quite like money.

So far it has been concerned mainly with the background of industrialization—power, communications, transport—and with the modernization of agriculture, itself a prerequisite of technical revolution. Its purpose has been to set the stage, provide the tools, help bring all its poor member States to the sort of condition that England was in before the gun went off at Huddersfield: and since its needy clients vary in their condition from near savagery to intellectual sublimity, this has required a catholic vision and an adaptable approach. Like the best of corporations, the World Bank often plays by ear, and is not hamstrung by its own charter. It has interpreted in several different ways, for example, a reference in that document to "sound business practices." It has often preferred to ignore the injunction that money should be lent only for specific projects (under the terms of the charter, cash may be lent in a more general way only "in special circumstances," an escape clause that the Bank has frequently in-

The Road to Huddersfield:

voked). Some loans are indeed for individual works. Some are passed to an intermediary development bank, to be dispersed at second hand. Some are merely injected into a nation's economy, to be diffused like a tonic in the bloodstream.

The absolute supremacy of the president within his organization means that he can direct its affairs as he likes, shift its emphasis this way or that, chop and change without the harassment of interfering committees or overbearing advisers. The Bank has many of the advantages of autocracy without the usual monolithic mediocrity. It need follow no blind ideology, fulfill no manifesto or unbending norm. It can examine each case on what is sometimes fondly called its merits (for in the early days especially, nations used to demand mammoth loans, not for any particular reason, but simply because that is what a bank is for: the first Chilean request for money was bound in black morocco). At H Street nothing need be inelastic. It all, as they say, depends.

The Bank makes loans at an average of two or three a month, and by the end of 1962 had made a total of 333 to 61 different countries. Not all of these were ignorant or even poor States. They included France, Denmark, Italy, Japan, Holland, Norway, and Australia. Most of the money, however, has gone to nations in the sweating tropical belt, that swathe of territory from Formosa to Peru which is still stertoriously laboring toward modernity. Most South American countries have had World Bank loans. Thirteen countries in Africa have benefited, twelve in Asia, and India has had twenty-three separate loans. Of the poor countries, India is by far the biggest recipient, followed by Japan, Australia, and Mexico. The geographical scale of the thing is superb, spanning the

A Journey to Five Continents

entire globe with the exception of North America, which needs no help, and the Soviet bloc, which scorns to ask for any. No private investment concern has ever surveyed so wide a spectrum; not even the great international corporations like Ford or Imperial Chemicals have had their fingers in such widely scattered pies; not even the greatest of the empires, the Roman or the British, sent their satraps and inspectors to quite such far-flung territories. No wonder Eugene Black, swiveling before his wall map, had to him an air not so much imperial as actually proprietorial.

The diversity of enterprises that this Bank has underwritten is scarcely less grandiose. Marginal its aid may be, but by now it is much the biggest international investment bank. The port of Bangkok was dredged with a World Bank loan, the city of Baghdad was freed from floods, the Cauca Valley in Colombia was electrified, the Northern Rhodesian railways were overhauled, the Icelandic radio transmitter was rehoused, the Ethiopian telephone system was reorganized, the Gabon manganese deposits were exploited, the Yugoslav timber industry was expanded, the Suez Canal was widened, the Australians were enabled to buy new airliners, the Dutch to build new ships, the Colombians to launch a regional development program, the Ceylonese to establish an institute of scientific research, the Turks to develop their private industry, the Panamanians to build grain silos. Wherever you go in the world, you may come across works into whose concrete, steel, or rubble the World Bank's bonds are woven: the great Yanhee Dam in Siam, one of the noblest structures in Asia; the Riesseck-Kreuzeck hydroelectric scheme in Austria; the vast new irrigation works of the Indus Basin; the nuclear

The Road to Huddersfield:

power station north of Naples; the pipeline that crosses the northern Sahara from Hassi Messaoud to the sea; the new iron-ore harbor in Mauretania; the tremendous Kariba Dam in the heartland of the Zambesi; the mill which, working twenty-four hours a day every day of the year, produces every single page of Chilean newsprint; roads in ten Latin American States, railways in four countries of Asia, sawmills in Finland, and bridges in Guatemala. From the power house in H Street, Washington, D.C., energies have found their way to some of the most distant of places, some of the strangest, and not a few of the stubbornest.

Far more important in a sense than these pulsating works are the attitudes they have helped to foster. Huddersfield is more than a town, more than a historical fact; it is also a frame of mind—an acceptance that old ways must go, a realization that new ones must be worked for. It has been the World Bank's prime contribution to progress, perhaps, to foster here and there the kind of outlook that can make the Huddersfield road less bumpy, less dangerous, less degrading to all its multitude of travelers. More important than steel for a factory is a manager to run it honestly. Harder to find than a new diesel locomotive is the resolution to maintain the track. Anyone can build you a power plant, but it takes maturity of mind to keep its turbines always turning, distribute its benefits fairly, foresee its best uses, and plan its proper expansion. All this is the concern of the World Bank, accounts for its sometimes starchy responses, and excuses its often lofty postures. It thinks it knows best, and by and large it does. It pretends to no idealist zeal, only to steady, sensible standards —money well used, money paid back. As the freethinker once remarked of the Almighty, "I don't always agree with Him, but at least He's consistent."

This, then, is one organization that is passing on the experience of Huddersfield and its peers of the West to the unmechanized parts of the earth. More than any other agent of contemporary history, it is consciously helping to spread the technical civilization into every corner of the earth—to remold mankind, you might say, in the western image. It is a complex organism, less simple by far than any medium of plain profit or political advantage, for it combines to a unique degree the reformist and the conservative qualities: reformist of intention, conservative of technique. It is rather like some aristocratic evangelist of the Victorian era, derided from the one side for his visionary views, from the other for his patrician manners, but nevertheless managing, side whiskers righteously quivering, to force his liberal statutes through a resentful but grudgingly respectful assembly.

The World Bank is, in a very real sense, a revolutionary force—as explosive in effect as any of those bubbling ferments and ambitions that heaved old England into the steam age. How varied is the soil in which its seeds germinate, how different are the numerous problems it has inherited from war, empire, and tradition, how exciting this motion of rebellion can be—and how lopsidedly the world rolls with its help toward the mills, we must now cross the continents to discover for ourselves.

⸝ 3 ⸜

Weird monarchy ⸝ pastoral integrity ⸝ Berghida ⸝ despotisms and discontents ⸝ omens of Huddersfield ⸝ bankers' yeast ⸝ too fast ⸝ L equals $\frac{rRP-(t+t')L}{i}$

IT IS ALL too easy to classify half the world as rich, half as poor, as our forebears used to split it neatly between Heathen and Believers. In fact there are as many grades of nationhood as there are of social nuance, and in the assembly of States, as in the women's club, you may meet the sophisticate and the ingenue, the *nouveaux riches* and the faded gentry, the affluent vulgar and the skin-flint demure. Even that part of the world which has patently not yet mechanized itself is a hodge-podge of varying maturity, and even inside individual countries there are often pockets of comfortable urbanity within wastelands of despair. If, however, we take Huddersfield as our watershed, then we may fit the emergent countries of the earth into apparent, if roughly contoured, gullies. It is not, of course, the steam age that these countries are preparing to enter: very often, like those Andean Indians, they have skipped that period of development altogether. It is not even the motor age, for, thanks to the effulgent energies of the West, many countries are perfectly familiar with the internal-combustion engine long before they reach their

The Road to Huddersfield:

moment of take-off. No, it is really the age of relief: the era when a people realizes that poverty, disease, and ignorance are not preordained and inescapable, but can be removed or palliated by the techniques of science.

Some countries of the contemporary world are far more primitive than England was at the time of the Industrial Revolution, for Huddersfield breaks sooner nowadays upon a developing comity. It is to such nations that the passion for change comes with most curdling and disturbing effect, much as the sudden onset of puberty disturbs a sensitive child; and nowhere is it occurring more theatrically than in the Empire of Ethiopia—high, proud, but bitter above the Horn of Africa. This weird but beguiling monarchy, poised in the highlands between the Nile and the Red Sea, has been one of the marvels and enigmas of geography throughout recorded history. Wonderfully isolated among its forbidding mountains, cut off from the trade routes of the ancients and the well-frequented channels of classical culture, Ethiopia long ago became a legend, one of the shimmering unknowns of hearsay, shrouded in rumor and tall story.

From Ethiopia the Queen of Sheba set out to Jerusalem, and to her shadowy court Solomon's own son went back as King, founding a dynasty whose monarchs still call themselves the Lions of Judah and claim all princely wisdom. This was the sort of place where dragons certainly be, and men with heads beneath their shoulders. This was the country of Prester John, that off-stage mogul of the Middle Ages, whose robes were woven by salamanders and laundered only in fire, who was attended always by seven kings, sixty dukes, thirty archbishops, twenty bishops, and 365 counts, who was descended from

Melchior, Caspar, and Balthazar, around whose hospitable table 30,000 knights could comfortably eat at one sitting, whose butler was an archbishop, whose groom was an archimandrite, and whose head chef was an eminent abbot. In Ethiopia the Fountain of Youth perpetually bubbled, beside the Sea of Aromatic Sand and the River of Precious Stones. In Ethiopia gigantic ants dug gold out of the sub-soil, and a number of unpopular tribes was walled up among the northern hills by order of Alexander the Great. Ethiopia was usually drawn mistily on the ancient maps, with phalanxes of spiky peaks, monstrous cloven-footed animals, and eerie giants; and her territories were usually left a little vague, for they were reliably supposed to extend westward from the sunrise, across the Three Indies and the Mountains of the Moon as far as the Tower of Babel.

Even when, in the sixteenth century, she emerged from the realms of golden fable into properly recorded experience, nothing about her was commonplace. Alone among the indigenous peoples of Africa, the Ethiopians were Christian, and it was this very fact that kept their country isolated and mysterious. "Encompassed on all sides," as Gibbon observed, "by the enemies of their religion, the Aethiopians slept near a thousand years, forgetful of the world by whom they were forgotten." The astonishing Monophysite Church of Ethiopia, imprisoned among its mountains, evolved a civilization all its own, a dream of round thatched churches and shuttered cloisters, crude but charming paintings, a lively literature, and a florid ritual. Ethiopia matured in war against her Muslim neighbors, in prayer and internecine slaughter at home, in a succession of warlike reigns. No enemies or strangers stayed

The Road to Huddersfield:

in this high fastness for long. A Portuguese Jesuit mission settled there for a time but was eventually expelled in ignominy. Sometimes Muslim marauders swept in and looted, but invariably withdrew. Once the British sent a punitive expedition up from the coast, complete with Lord Napier and a squadron of elephants, but its red-coated columns soon lumbered home again, taking with them only a cache of priceless manuscripts and the Imperial Crown (later returned to the Ethiopians by King George V of England). In 1889 an Italian invasion army was not merely humiliated but actually castrated, and even Mussolini's occupation of the country lasted only six years. Few States on earth have preserved their independence so long or their character more tenaciously.

The domestic history of Ethiopia is no less gaudy, tragic, and enthralling. One Ethiopian Emperor, faced with political ignominy, shot himself through the roof of the mouth. Another decided that he was not descended from Solomon at all but from the Prophet Mohammed, and had to be shut away in a gilded cage for the rest of his life. Many died violently, some went mad, nearly all were embroiled in ceaseless rivalries and intrigues, sometimes feline, sometimes volcanic. So full-blooded indeed was the royal strain that in 1800 there were six vociferous claimants to the throne. Nevertheless, through all these perilous vicissitudes, Ethiopia remained a unity, and in fact extended her hegemony, if not as far as the sunrise, at least into many Muslim territories round about. Her flavor was preserved partly by its own strength, partly by topography, partly by the very backwardness of the place. She was never a colony for long, never even an arena of investment, and though she possesses highland farming country as fine as any-

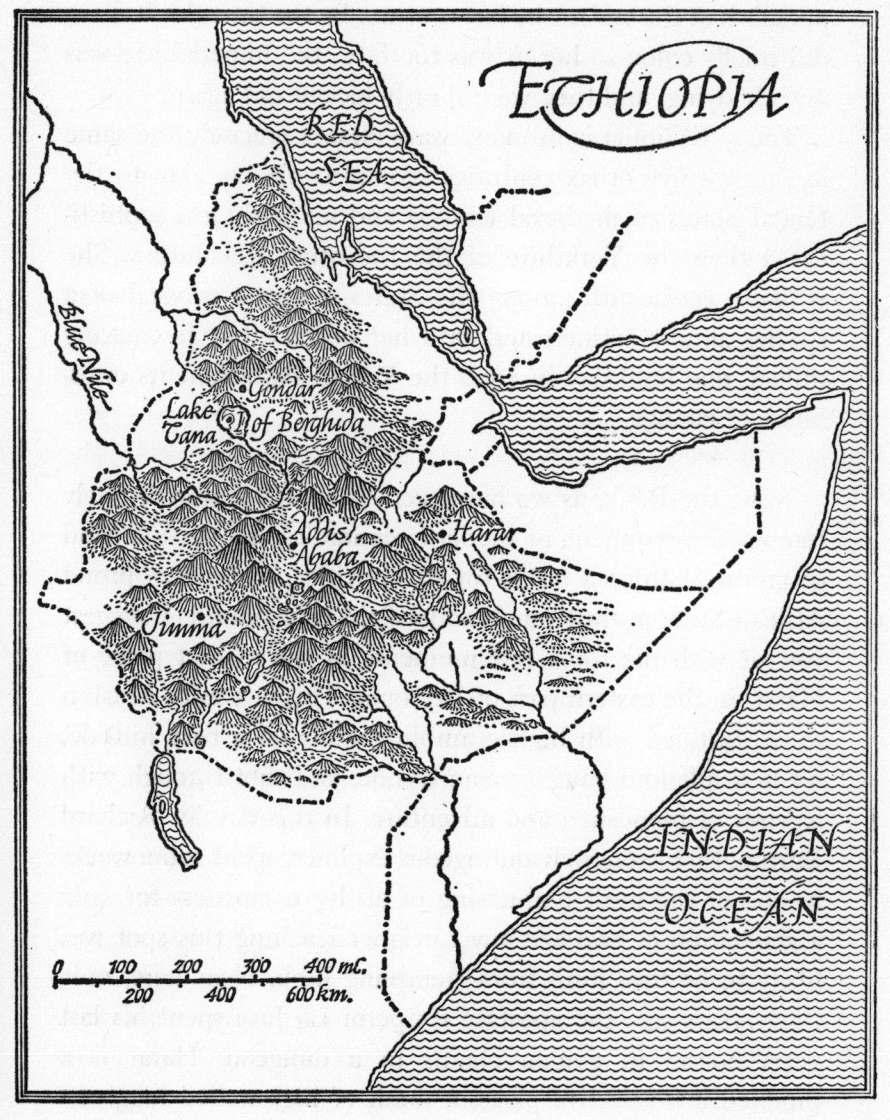

The Road to Huddersfield:

thing in Kenya, she escaped the onslaughts of European imperialism at the end of the last century. By the time the Italians did briefly colonize her, it was too late: the imperial age was already dying, and they were shortly kicked out again.

Today Ethiopia is in many ways almost precisely the same as she was five or six centuries ago: recognizably akin to the feudal States of medieval Europe and infinitely less sophisticated than the Yorkshire of the Industrial Revolution. She is like a coelacanth among the States, a proud survival of a species almost extinct; and into her obscure but fascinating milieu, one bold day in 1950 the World Bank sent its emissaries of change.

Now, the Bank, as we have seen, is a high-powered, finely tempered instrument of modern economics. To see the kind of ground Ethiopia offers for its activities, to set this proud African State against our Huddersfield background, I suggest you sit with me for a few moments in the market place of Harar, in the eastern part of Ethiopia. This is a lofty Muslim town, fortified with high crumbling walls on a bare hillside, set in a splendid haughty countryside, and shot through with legends of bloodshed and adventure. In this city Sir Richard Burton, that supremely outrageous explorer, spent some weeks in one of the most hair-raising of all his escapades—for only a generation or two ago any foreigner reaching this spot was likely to be torn limb from trembling limb. Near here, only thirty years ago, the apostate Emperor Lij Jasu spent his last years bound in golden chains in a dungeon. Harar is a jumbled introspective place, a mesh of high-walled higgledy-piggledy lanes, a clutter of rambling mud houses; and in the evening, if you stand very still beside the city walls, you may see the prowling hyenas slink out of the dust like mangy hump-backed foxes.

In the very heart of this antique entity stands the market, one of the most interesting I have ever seen. If you sit down there on a friendly doorstep beside a grave-faced silversmith tapping and chiseling away outside his open-fronted shop, with a fringe of beard waggling around his chin and the lurking suspicion of a twinkle in his eye—if you settle there beside his bench, as he nods you a courteous and preoccupied welcome and adds another infinitesimal link to the fragile silver chain he is fashioning, then you may taste with a piquant pleasure the state of modern Ethiopia. Never was there a market more lively, more varied, more glistening. Here are the wild-eyed Somali sages, wiry as panthers, all fuzzy hair and togas, striding by with their staves like burning hermits. Here are the slender Galla girls, half naked and exquisitely assured, with hair elaborately braided and figures swathed in blinding cottons. Here are tough Negroid women with urchin haircuts and flimsy white dresses like honeymoon nightgowns; and adorable bald plump babies, peering large-eyed from hammocks slung on many a black shiny back; and thin-faced, hawk-nosed merchants of Arab strain, like wizards or sorcerers in the hubbub; and a thousand small barefoot children, perpetually scampering lightly down the stone-strewn alleys and through the cluttered stalls.

There are mounds of vivid vegetables everywhere, and stacks of steaming meat, and trays of glittering baubles, and gay rolls of cotton and calico, and bouncy sniffing little dogs beneath your feet, and a blazing African sky above your head, and

The Road to Huddersfield:

always that earnest craftsman at your side, tinkling and thumping at his tiny anvil, or engaged in determined but desultory haggling with virtually nude but otherwise impeccable debutantes. There is nothing ugly to be seen there, nothing pretentious, nothing crudely mass-produced, nothing vulgar or abashed. Nobody jostles you, or sneers, or mocks your outlandish costume. It is like watching an assembly of lovely lithe-limbed animals, so easily do all those people move, so naturally, so discreetly. These are the noble savages of legend, children of the thatched hut and the empty place, sisters of specious innocence; and they represent in their every gesture, in every keen eye and rippling muscle, all that the technical revolution must inevitably destroy.

You may find such people still, sometimes heavily disguised, in many unexpected parts of the earth: among the leathery Lapps of northern Sweden, the grotesquely folksy farmers of the Tyrol, even in the United States itself, if you penetrate behind the tourist folk rites to the dusty heart of the Navajo country. In Ethiopia, though, nearly everyone is as simple as this, and the market place at Harar is not a picturesque anachronism but the norm. Here the World Bank is dealing with one of the most backward of all the States, one of the very furthest from Huddersfield, and a couple of miles from any Ethiopian highway, you find yourself virtually back in the Middle Ages of Europe.

Ethiopian manners still smack of knightly chivalry: the sweeping bow, the formal kiss, the handshake that lasts a whole conversation, the protracted exchanges of stylized politesse—"How have you passed the night? Thanks be to God! What is the state of your harvest? Praise God!" The Ethiopians are still a hauntingly handsome race, like figures on an Assyrian bas-relief, or pottery Etruscans. I can still see the face of a merchant I once watched weighing millet in one of the Ethiopian markets. His wife sat loyally at his side, wearing a long white tunic and a sort of string mobcap, and three or four laborers in raggedy jerkins hastened about with sacks and hoarse exclamations. The merchant sat on a kitchen chair as grand as any Prester John, bowing solemnly over his scales with an air of fathomless probity; when he looked up at me, I saw flaming black eyes sunk deep beneath high cheekbones, a nose etched like steel, a mouth at once commanding and sensitive, gray hair curling Homerically about his temples, a look cold with authority but salted with dry, knowing, patrician humor. He caught my eye and allowed himself the thinnest flickering quiver of a smile, and as he did so he slammed the lock of his scales with a gesture fearfully final, as though he had ordered the instant expulsion of the Jesuits, or had just decapitated his own grandfather.

Ethiopia is full of faces just as striking, just as suggestive: the distant tranced faces of bearded priests above the great silver crosses that dangle on their chests: the resigned biblical faces of the old men who loiter, leaning agilely on knobby sticks, outside any church, law court, or great man's house; the quick, wary faces of the educated youngbloods; the aloof, uncurious faces of the Muslims, performing their ablutions in their flagged courtyards; the gentle, vacuous, disturbing faces of the young prostitutes, in virginal white or vicarage embroidery, who gossip through the dusk hours outside their dim-lit sidewalk boudoirs. This is Africa with Semitic overtones, alight always with intelligence. These are not the coarse, jolly faces of Lagos or Accra. Here there is something more in the blood, something that puts me in mind of the black nobles of antiquity, the slender Negro gondoliers of Carpaccio's Venice, or the Ethiop king at the stable door. More than anywhere else in Africa, here you may feel the legendary nobility of this continent, the sense of ebony style that so bemused the old chroniclers.

The Ethiopians have a rich and living literary language—Amharic—with thirty-three letters written in 231 different ways. They have an ancient tradition of sacred painting, at once delightfully naïve and insidiously subtle. They have their own calendar, the Era of Mercy, in which the year begins on September 11 (1962 in the western calendar was 1954 in Ethiopia). They have their own roster of saints, some of whom are honored in festivals not just once a year but once a month. Above all, they still have a powerful (if decadent) Church, which largely sets the tone of the Empire to this day.

Wonderfully varied is the society which this rooted and idiosyncratic culture has cherished. Ethiopia really is an Empire, in fact as in protocol. The people called the Amharas, from the northern and central highlands of the country, have imposed their rule upon an astonishing gallimaufry of other peoples, tribes, and religions, but beneath their Monophysite sway, many another manner of life survives. There are millions of Muslims in Ethiopia, and thousands of black Jews, and folk who believe in the deity called Wak, whose eye is the sun, and animists of diverse curious ritual, and struggling Catholics, and inert but cheerful pagans. There are jet-black Ethiopians, and brown, and Ethiopians almost white. There are people who live in round mud houses, and people who live in square stone houses, and people who do not live in houses at all but incessantly roam the wastelands with their herds of goats and camels.

There are some Ethiopians who honor the suzerainty of the Sultan of Aussa, and others who obey the Diglal of the Beni Amer, and still more who are subject to the hereditary Nazir of the Ad Sheik. There are the nearly naked Danakil, and the people around Lake Abaya, who live on hippopotamus meat, and the fierce nomads of the Red Sea littoral, who, only in 1960, raided a passing train like screaming Apaches, murdering several of its passengers. There are Semites in Ethiopia, and Hamites, and Cushites, and people the anthropologists describe as being "dolichocephalic, prognathous Nilotic types." There are people of many a proud local patriotism—the Gallas, the Somalis, the Sidama, the Saho. There are people who speak Bilen or Beja, Tigre or Tigrinya, Arabic or Chaha, Harari or Awiya, Sidamo or Kambatta, Hadya or Amharic or even Kunama, a language that has no known connection with any other tongue on the lips of men. There really is a place called Bonka. The people called Jam-Jams are easily recognizable, I am creditably assured, by their leather tam-o'-shanters.

The spectacle of such a country must have been daunting indeed when the logical rationalists of the World Bank first set foot in Ethiopia. It was their first venture into Africa, and it must have been a far, sad cry indeed from the pleasing telephone manner of H Street. It is a marvelous thing, all the same, to see a country of such absolute pastoral integrity. This is still one of the least-known of the earth's corners, one of the few places where aventurers of the old school may saddle their mules and camels and wander merrily off into nowhere,

The Road to Huddersfield:

still with a sporting chance that some wild brigand may assault them out of the sun. I was once meandering along the northern short of Lake Tana, the great gray sea that gives rise to the Blue Nile, when I noticed across a narrow spit of water a small green wooded island, lying silent and seductive among the reeds. As I stood there gazing at it and wondering how I could get across the strait, there appeared out of nowhere a smiling, light-footed boatman, a Semite of infinite slim delicacy, wearing practically nothing at all except the silver cross that dangled around his neck. Without a word, but with gestures suggestive and faunlike, he led me to his craft, a precarious reed canoe hidden there among the rushes: and in a moment or two I stood damp but delighted upon the islet of Berghida (for the Tana boats do not even aim at watertightness, floating as they do by the buoyancy of their separate reeds).

It is a very small island, tangled with thick foliage, dark but sunlit, like a little Zanzibar or a less accessible Tobago—the sort of place Oberon might retire to if ever the tourists ruined his wood. And in fact it is a magic spot, for Berghida is one of the holy islands of Tana, a place of immemorial and inviolable sanctity. Its only inhabitants are a group of hermits and a presiding priest, and no woman has ever set foot there, nor any female beast. Swift and airily my guide led me to the heart of this strange place, moving himself so lightly that he looked as though he were riding the lake breeze: and presently we found, lounging rather despondently among a circle of round mud huts, the holy men of Berghida—eight torpid but amiable anchorites, growing old in isolation.

They gave me a plate piled high with hot black beans, and

a tin bowl of cold green soup; and I gave them an orange, some buns, two bananas, and a bottle of Ethiopian Chianti —an esoteric but palatable vintage; and so we sat there together talking, laughing, and drinking, while my faun leapt gracefully from hermit to hermit, nibbling a banana, sometimes pressing some more of the soup on me, sometimes urging a laughing elder to another sip of Chianti, and the youngest of those holy men sang to us in a peculiar falsetto voice, like the whining of wind in rigging. The grasses grew tall and lush around us. The sky was a pale watery blue. The softest of African breezes sprang off the lake. To the north I could see the dun coastline of the Jalo promontory, speckled with tough shrubbery and haunted by loping baboons; to the south the waters of Tana stretched bland and peaceful, bounded by the volcanic humps of the Debra Tabor hills. Around us the little island lay in a hush of sensual privacy, disturbed only by the buzzing of its indefatigable insects and the squawking of its improbable birds. It was a moment of exotic idyll. It was the kind of occasion you could enjoy only in the backward regions, the unredeemed, the laggards on the Huddersfield road, whose horizons are still smokeless and whose holy men still eat beans and cold green soup on unfrequented islands.

All over Ethiopia you may enjoy such experiences, whether you are among the ferocious desert wanderers of the south or the magnificent patriarchs of the Amharic uplands. Ethiopia still possesses an inner mystery and allure, as she did in the days when the geographers called her simply "The Land of God": and I defy any man of sensibility, even an economist or a gloomy statistician, to stand on the Red Sea shore and see her mountains towering there, silent and sealed in cloud,

The Road to Huddersfield:

without a tremor of excitement—nicely tempered, if he is wise, with tactful apprehension.

Well, you may say, no rising expectations there, no need to illuminate the choices. Leave well enough alone, and send the World Bank somewhere else. Certainly the first question that will cross your mind, as you follow the Bank's trail through this tortuous society, is whether Ethiopia really ought to be helped toward the mills: whether it is necessary, whether it is desirable, whether indeed it is possible. But you will presently be convinced, I think, that even here, in this bastion of old orders, the idyl is fading. This is a country rich in resources and reserves, where nobody is starving and only a small minority is politically coherent: yet only a scratch behind the feathered panoply, only a sniff around the Harar market, will persuade you, not only of the will to change, but even of its necessity.

I have spent only three days in Gondar, the ancient capital of the Ethiopian kings, which flaunts its splendid castle ruins in the moorlands north of Tana. Only three short days, yet in that time I saw the feet of a grandee kissed by his prostrate serfs, I tried to comfort five poor souls savaged by a mad hyena, I followed a pair of manacled prisoners through the main street of the city, I raised my hat to a nabob before whose briskly trotting mule, kicking up the back-street dust, a retainer with a big stick stumbled in sweating barefoot heraldry. I was importuned by limbless beggars. I was entertained by illiterate priests. When I dropped my notebook in the street, I had to bribe some soldiers of the garrison to give it back again.

Ethiopia is not all Arcady. The sinuous primitives are lovely to watch, like gazelles and leopards out of the veldt, but behind the splendor, much is squalid. The people are scabbed in sickness and blinkered in ignorance; perhaps 90% of them are illiterate. To this day there is only a handful of qualified Ethiopian doctors, and the vast majority of this citizenry never goes to school at all. The resources of the country are not properly used, and most of Ethiopia is still so inaccessible that you can get there only by atrociously difficult mule-back journeys. Nobody knows how many Ethiopians there are. It is a rare Ethiopian who knows how old he is. The Danakil tribesmen of the Red Sea shore still measure their manhood by the number of enemies they have killed and emasculated.

Socially and politically Ethiopia is sadly stunted: one of the most archaic of all the dizzily variegated States that can boast membership of the Bank. This is a kingdom of traditional despotism, ruled still by an Emperor who claims descent from Solomon and possibly even Cush. Haile Selassie is an old man now, but the compulsion of his regal character is undimmed, and the very first thing that strikes the stranger in Ethiopia is the presence of the Emperor, King of Kings, Elect of God, Conquering Lion of the Tribe of Judah, with his Minister of the Pen and his Mouth of the King, his haughty palace lion and his fierce festooned bodyguard. He rules his kingdom as a patriarchal autocrat, and his presence pervades everything, from the foreign policy to the street names. He has an eye on every activity, an ear at almost every door. Nearly every institution seems to bear his name, nearly every conversation, sooner or later, leads up to his character. Half the men of authority are his relatives, and most of the rest his nominees.

The Road to Huddersfield:

If you stay at the Ghion Hotel in Addis Ababa you are staying at his property; if you ask for some hotel writing-paper, it has been printed on his presses; if you read a newspaper over breakfast, he controls it; if you raise your eyes for a moment's meditation, you will almost certainly find them resting upon a portrait of the King of Kings, glittering in ceremonial fineries or bravely austere in khaki. There are fewer telephones per head in Ethiopia than there are in almost any other country: yet in the Addis telephone book there are forty-five numbers for the Imperial Bodyguard and forty-nine for the Imperial Palaces, including the Chariot and Vehicle Department, the Assistant Garage Chief's Residence, and a chamber ambivalently described as the Grand Palace Rest Room. ("Chief of Staff of His Imperial Majesty," runs one entry in this fascinating directory, and adds respectfully: "See *Special* Chief of Staff of His Imperial Majesty.") In Ethiopia the Emperor is Everywhere, with a capital E, for never was a Hapsburg more mindful of protocol or more jealous of the royal "We." "*L'Etat,*" as Haile Selassie would doubtless prefer to have it said, "*c'est Nous.*"

His is an empire of the old kind, an organism nearer to Shakespeare's history plays than to Huddersfield's orderly ledgers. It is a complex and rambling affair, strained always by violent centrifugal forces. Only a few Ethiopians have any sense of nationality, and many a proud satrap demands allegiances of his own. Several powerful internal energies pose potential threats to the emperors of Ethiopia, from the Church itself, with its mystic hold over half the populace, to the motions of regional separatism implicit in a commonwealth of such kaleidoscopic variety. All must be locked in discipline to keep the State from falling apart, and this the Emperor has achieved by employing the techniques of a medieval police state. Secret police are ubiquitous. Hangings are often public. Politics are ferociously prohibited. Trade unions may not exist. The security of the Empire is maintained by traditional methods of autocracy—summary arrests, exile to distant badlands, some say torture. The daily press is entirely official, and lick-spittle at that. Books even vestigially critical of the regime are proscribed, and citizens are often chary of talking to strangers about the condition of the land. The constitution, in principle impeccable, is in practice half meaningless. You can be sent to prison without trial, or sacked from your job without explanation. From top to bottom of this nation you may recognize the European Middle Ages, from the semidivine nature of the kingship to the social structure of the countryside, whose pattern of great man, tenant, and serf is almost precisely the shape of European feudalism seven or eight centuries ago.

We cannot blame the Ethiopians for all this, and indeed there is to their ornate traditionalism a lingering fragrance of pathos. It reminds me a little of the Hawaiian monarchy, a forlorn but lovable institution, whose kings set great store by orbs and scepters and decked themselves in the feathers of the o-o bird. To most such patriarchal, pastoral societies there is a great deal of charm, whether it is expressed in the gorgeous gardens of Tuscan dukes or the exquisite foibles of Kyoto—pictures of Fujiyama that fall into correct perspective only when you kneel on the floor before them, floor boards whose squeaks are attuned to reproduce the songs of bush warblers. The Ethiopian monarchy, with its attendant patrician

The Road to Huddersfield:

orders, is sometimes heedless and sometimes cruel, but never without dignity.

Thanks to its lofty resolution, Ethiopia has never sunk into that bog of crossed values and half-cock politics that has overcome most of Africa. This is still a lovely and impressive country, "a feast for the sight and a charm for the mind," like England before the industrial apocalypse. The people retain a self-respect that sometimes borders upon arrogance, and to the world the name of Ethiopia still spells independence, pride, and fascination. What is more, by the standards of such an antediluvian society the ruling heirarchy really has made concessions to progress. There is the beginning of a parliamentary system, and a proper civil service is, in fits, starts, and delusions, spasmodically being organized. The growth of education, pitifully limited though it is, must represent to the Emperor and his kind liberality of almost reckless goodwill—just as the Education Acts of the nineteenth century seemed to generations of English gentlemen.

But despite it all—or perhaps because of it—Ethiopia is a country of discontent. After millennia of isolation, she has glimpsed the other side, and wherever sophistication has touched the Ethiopians, however lightly, wherever the edge of the curtain has slipped aside, there you will meet disgruntlement and the will to change. Almost despite herself, Ethiopia is creeping towards the mills. She is not all shuttered in anomaly, for all her Gondar lepers and Berghida hermits. Addis Ababa itself, for instance, has recognizably sidled into the twentieth century. To be sure, there are still goats in its streets by day, and scavenging hyenas at night. There is a vast seething market place, the biggest in all Africa, where you may buy mule trappings or Coptic manuscripts, eat the searing peppered food of the people, or have yourself measured for a goatskin cloak. There are hovels and donkeys in Addis still, and pitiful lepers, and bureaucrats of timeless procrastination. Nevertheless, this is a city that has sniffed the odors of progress. Through the slums the palsied beggars crawl on blistered knees, but down the road the children of the elite stream fresh and fragrant out of the Lycée. There are gay little coffee shops about, and movie houses, and an elegant restaurant or two, and several hospitals, and even a university. Addis is a gateway on that road across the moors, and through its portals change is entering Ethiopia—in troika, as always, with hope and grievance.

It is partly the presence of foreigners that is fermenting this country. Since the Italian invasion in 1935 Ethiopia has been full of them. Some are businessmen, working on their own account. Some represent the United Nations or Point Four, the British Council or La Maison Française. Some are employed by the Ethiopian government. Some do not seem to be employed at all, but are just wandering about collecting silver trinkets or writing books. You cannot escape them. There are Russians building a technical college, Americans planning a university, Britons advising the State Bank, Indians training the Imperial bodyguard, Swedes installing telephones, Norwegians reorganizing the navy, Yugoslavs building a cotton mill, Israelis making roads. There is an American special adviser to the Emperor, and a British legal counselor. There are foreigners in nearly every ministry and nearly every hospital. There are French, American, and English schools. There are the vast offices of the United Nations Economic Commission

The Road to Huddersfield:

for Africa, stuffed with intellectuals of a dozen nationalities. Addis Ababa is, as the speculators say, wide open, and through the lens or focus of their capital the Ethiopians have glimpsed the distant mills and see their pastoral kingdom clearer.

More pertinently still, it is education that has set Ethiopia in fitful motion. Where there is a school, there is a new perspective. A growing new generation of Ethiopians is no longer satisfied with old levels of living, old values of caste and opportunity. Thousands realize, as they watch their luckier brothers learn to read and write, that a world without letters is a migraine world—half blotted out. Thousands more, as they dip into the intoxicating delights of literature, history, and science, grasp for the first time how stultified their fathers' lives have been, how arid, how crippled. Most significantly of all, hundreds of young Ethiopians have been sent abroad for their education, to Harvard or Cambridge, Heidelberg or the Sorbonne, and come back with a new vision, like men returning into twilight out of the afternoon.

You can hardly conceive, from the blasé vantage point of a literate society, how sizzling is the interest incited by education in such a country as this, how hungrily, like addicts of some heady stimulant, the poor peoples grasp and absorb it, what an excitement it is to them, what a delight. It is three centuries since Shakespeare observed his schoolboy creeping like snail unwillingly to school: but in most of the world, even today, going to school is a privilege indeed. The shining morning faces that gaze back at you out of an Ethiopian classroom, with their burning eyes and gleaming teeth, their brows furrowed with the effort of comprehension, their fingers clenched on their pencils with a taut intensity—the faces of these schoolchildren reflect not a trace of reluctance but more the kind of ecstasy an American child displays upon receiving his first motorcycle, or an English boy as he swings toward silly mid-off with his brand-new cricket bat.

Frustration is the immediate result, and malcontent. There are far more white-collar workers than there are white-collar jobs. There are not enough schools for avid pupils. Men who have lived three long glorious years at Cambridge return to all the squalor, ignorance, and inequity of an almost medieval environment. Young hopefuls who have tasted the fun, ease, and efficiency of a technical society return to the mule trails and the eye of Wak. The Ethiopian fighter pilot, swinging like a lean black god toward his American jet, feels himself a fish out of water, and the aspirant politician, stifled by the old-school discipline of the system, considers himself to be cruelly oppressed.

It is an old story, of course. You may hear the same arguments of frustration all over the world, from Ecuador to Formosa, even among the angry young men of England herself —wherever the state of society seems to snaffle the hopes of a rising generation. For the first time there are angry young men in Ethiopia, too, not just cross-patch potentates. The old order is doomed at last, for the people are beginning to know that there need be no lepers in the market place, no sweating outrunner before the grandee's mule, no ignorant poverty in a country of abundance. Tradition still stands cap-a-pie, as severe as any De Coverley when the yokels omitted to tug their forelocks; but just as the yokels presently learned better, so progress is just beginning to threaten the structure of Ethiopian society.

The Road to Huddersfield:

I was once standing outside the Jubilee Palace in Addis Ababa when the Emperor Haile Selassie, in a convoy of American limousines, swept out into the city. Instantly the atmosphere around me was horribly bewitched. Huge bodyguards with Tommy guns leaped into the road, halting the passing traffic and pushing the bystanders aside. A gray Land-Rover, bristling with automatic weapons, skidded through the gates in the royal wake. A half-crazed beggar boy, whining an appeal to his Emperor, was hijacked brusquely out of the way. The people beside me bowed low as the big cars passed, the Emperor's small shape deep in the padded shadows of his seat; but to me, the flavor of that moment, at once acrid, defiant, and forlorn, suggested only a long, slow farewell to Prester John and his abbot chef, and the first distant wail of the factory hooter. Only a decade earlier, after all, those folk on the sidewalk would have thrown themselves flat on their faces.

Thus even Ethiopia edges toward the mills. The symptoms are, amoeba-like, sluggishly cohering. I do not mean that she can instantly, in some dazzling eruption of national vigor, transform herself into an industrial society; I mean that the circumstances are just beginning to combine that will ease her out of a predominant past into a predominant future. She can legitimately look forward to a moment when, instead of being largely static, she will be in a perpetual condition of growth: making more things, growing more crops, eating more food, owning more possessions, learning more, knowing more, seeing more, understanding more, traveling more, earning more, spending more, thinking more, and possibly regretting more. She is indescribably backward today, but in a world of abrupt transitions and truncated processes, she can expect an astonishing change in her manner of life within, say, the next generation.

What are the signs of this impending event? It sounds a little like astrology, the conjunction of planets or Sagittarius rising. There are, though, portents less celestial. First, the economists and the historians agree that essential to the process of evolution is a widening of horizons, such as the English experienced as their merchants scoured the oceans in search of trade, and their young men went out to govern distant dependencies or counter the rebuffs of impudent minutemen. This extension of vision comes more easily nowadays, as we have seen, through the medium of press, film, and travel, and even in Ethiopia you may now sense the first glimmerings of the new awareness.

Second, the pundits declare that some historical catalyst is necessary to the evolution, some firing of national energy: in Germany the rise of patriotic feeling, in Communist Russia the revolution, in India the achievement of independence. In Ethiopia, we need hardly doubt, this impetus will be provided someday by a change in the political and social system, the end of patriarchal despotism after so many centuries of autarchy, the fresh start that will eventually be made by the "youngmen," to borrow the splendid Ghanaian generification for anyone imaginative and on the move.

Third, there must be money. It has been said that to propel a nation into a condition of growth, into the action of expansion, a minimum of 12% of the national income must be invested in a productive way: either there must be a flow

The Road to Huddersfield:

of cash from outside, or enough citizens must be induced to plow their funds into the economy instead of squandering it on gewgaws, rough shoots, castles, or Riviera dalliances. In particular, money must be used to create the background of Huddersfield: the roads, banks, and warehouses, the schools and the institutions, the managers, the technicians, and the middlemen.

It is in satisfying the last two criteria that such an institution as the World Bank can help such a country as Ethiopia. It cannot be claimed that many enterprising foreign businessmen have sunk their fortunes in this State. Before the Italian invasion, alien enterprises were few indeed. The French, at the end of the nineteenth century, built a railway from Addis Ababa to the Somaliland coast, but this was largely a gesture of imperial flamboyance, chiefly intended to sustain the French port of Djibouti. For the rest, until Anno XIIII of the Fascist era, almost the only foreign businessmen in Ethiopia were obscure White Russians and miscellaneous adventurers of the sort Mr. Evelyn Waugh epitomized so meticulously in *Black Mischief* and *Scoop*—Erik Olafson, for example, who was not only Swedish Vice-Consul and head surgeon at the Mission Hospital, but also proprietor of the combined Tea, Bible, and Chemist Shop. Behind the Italian armies, though, there entered an active cadre of colonists, determined to make of Ethiopia what the British further south had made of Kenya, and their contribution to the national progress was more valuable than most Ethiopians like to admit.

Thanks largely to them, there does exist the nucleus of a commercial system, an acquaintance with modern banking methods and means of exchange. There is the beginning of an industrial sector: Ethiopian factories already make fabrics, cement, sugar, salt, shoes, beer, beeswax, buttons, carpets, hats, paint, soap, and (of course) spaghetti. What roads there are were mostly built by the Italians. What readiness there is to risk the profits of the land in the uncertainties of industry is mostly an ironic by-product of imperialism. This embryo structure of modernism the World Bank has tried to strengthen by hastening the growth of investment, now that the Ethiopians are their own masters again. One of its loans to Ethiopia has financed a Development Bank—a channel through which loans can be made to any kind of private project, from a sawmill to a nylon plant. It is hoped that by such small grafted beginnings, Ethiopia will be urged toward self-growth, toward the moment when the process of expansion "takes," like a cutting or a vaccination, becomes self-engendering and cumulative, and boosts the nation at last into the technical age. Twelve per cent, they say, is the minimum for such a consummation. Though Ethiopia is nowhere near there yet —3.7% is the latest estimate, compared with perhaps 5% for England in 1688—still, the Bank reasons, every bit helps.

The second contribution the Bank has made has been to help improve communications. Their telephone service has been rebuilt, and an Imperial Telecommunications Board established under Swedish management. There are still only about 12,000 receivers in the whole Empire, but the system has been greatly improved with new equipment and new techniques, and now offers many fancy refinements (for the equivalent of twenty cents you can have summoned to the telephone, in theory anyway, any individual who lives within six miles of an instrument—though the delay might be excessive, I suspect, if you happened to want to speak to one of the Berghida hermits). This is a far cry from the beginnings of the Ethiopian telephone system, in 1903, when people used to think that if they got too close to the wires the Emperor would not only hear what they were saying but actually see their wicked faces.

The Bank has also helped to improve the roads, a task crucial to Ethiopian development. The Italians built some excellent highways in Ethiopia, but most of them have rotted and crumbled into dereliction. Until a year or two ago, there were virtually no tarmac roads outside the cities: all was bumps, gaps, and landslides. Indeed, as we have seen, most of Ethiopia is still absolutely inaccessible to motor traffic; only the hardiest of mule-back travelers, for example, can visit the fabulous rock churches of Lalibela, which ought to be one of the great tourist spectacles of the world. If it were not for the American-managed State airline, whose aircraft are painted a brilliant orange, most of the Empire would be as remote today as it was in the Dark Ages (it still takes nearly three weeks for a coffee caravan to reach Addis from Jimma, where the crop is grown). This state of affairs the World Bank has greatly improved by making two loans to the Ethiopian Highway Department, which is now hard at work, under American guidance, in all four corners of the kingdom.

Most tellingly, though, the Bank hopes to help Ethiopia by the force of example. In particular, it likes to think that the Telecommunications Board, which was set up as a condition of aid, will be a sort of pilot institution, to establish a standard for the future and to act as a core of technical efficiency around which public attitudes can cohere. The Board has certainly set an example in its treatment of employees, who are given free medical care, for example, and proper coffee breaks, and are generally treated as intelligent adults. It employs many women, an innovation in Shangri-La. It recruits its technicians during their junior year at high school, and thus offers a boy a career before he has time to get frustrated. It is a kind of germ of modernity in the body of Ethiopia.

So does a brewer drop a little yeast into the hops to set his barrel bubbling.

Has the application of foreign money and means to this haughty and archaic monarchy been a success? Since you ask, not altogether. The World Bank is not terribly proud of its achievements in Ethiopia, its first African client, and the Ethiopians are not always complimentary about the World Bank. It has been a tiresome honeymoon. In particular, it has demonstrated how *long* it takes to shift a nation's gears, what an agonizingly muddled process the adjustment can be, and how expensive a commodity is time. Most of the foreign technicians have now left the Telecommunications Board, but it will probably be another decade before the Ethiopians can run it all by themselves. The Development Bank has been operating for ten years, but to this day only an infinitesimal fraction of the Ethiopian population understands what modern business is all about.

Basically, and paradoxically, this is because the pace is too fast. Nobody has much choice in the timing of history, but it would really be better for everyone if the motion of the

Ethiopian body politic could be retarded, to allow its several limbs to move in time. The demands of the coherent Ethiopians cannot long be denied, and it is in fact they who dictate the progress of the State; but the fact remains that while at one end of the national spectrum a handful of sophisticated young Ethiopians is perfectly able to manage a bank, run a factory, or fly a supersonic jet, at the other end most of the populace scarcely understands the meaning of money.

There has been none of the long, steady, almost imperceptible approach to maturity that characterized European history before the Industrial Revolution—the Bible classes that fostered literacy, the progressively more liberal legislation, the overseas adventuring that cherished commerce, the gradual marshaling of resources and adjustment of attitudes. In Ethiopia, most people live by simple barter: in the more accessible country parts you may swap a bag of beans for a bottle of pink nail polish, but elsewhere values, commodities, methods, and all have remained unaltered for centuries, and if a sack of salt would buy you a cow in your great-great-grandfather's time, so it will today. The Deputy Governor of the Ethiopian State Bank is as civilized, cultured, and well-read a man as you can meet anywhere in the world; but if you look at the electric light switch in the anteroom to his office, where the messengers assemble, you will see that all around it they have imprinted, in a revealing brown pastiche, a myriad grubby fingerprints, signatures of a still childlike society.

For the whole texture of this place is alarmingly worn and thin to bear the impact of the new modernity. Not enough is known about the country, and the State pitifully lacks expertise and statistical analysis. Land tenure, for example, is so inextricably confused that nobody alive really understands it, and agriculture there can never be modernized without land reform. The Church owns perhaps a third of the land, the Emperor another third, and the rest is sunk in a morass of customary claims, feudal tenures, litigious disputes, sharecropping, public rights, wasteland, and nomadic usage. The Ethiopian Development Bank once had loan applications from two men both claiming to own the same field: when its assessors delved into the conflict, they found that the property really belonged to a third citizen, who promptly applied for a loan himself.

Similarly, the imperial attitude toward development, which is distinctly proprietorial, is scarcely adjusted to the Huddersfield focus. Haile Selassie, once finding himself dissatisfied with a decision of the Chamber of Deputies, instantly summoned that entire legislature up to the palace to put them right: and it is with a kindred avuncular but peremptory interest that he has surveyed the economic progress of his Empire. The Highway Authority, whose job it is to build the great trunk roads of the kingdom, has repeatedly been diverted into building parking places for the royal palaces, approach roads to princely retreats, foundations for airstrips. Twice the Swedish managers of the Telecommunications Board have resigned because the government, which knows less about telephones than a camel knows about water-skiing, has arbitrarily interfered with its affairs. So testy and protracted were the disputes surrounding the establishment of this body that it was three years after the signing of the World Bank loan agreement before the money was actually handed over, and when the new buildings were completed, seven years later,

The Road to Huddersfield:

the government refused to pay the construction companies.

As for the poor Development Bank, it has fought an uphill battle. It has been authoritatively described as "a lousy bank," anyway, and so cavalier have its clients been toward it that legal action has been brought against at least eight debtor companies. When I was in Addis Ababa I met the recently appointed general manager of this institution, a sanguine German. He seemed to be approaching his new duties in a spirit of cheerful assurance, as though he were merely taking over an outlying branch of the Deutsche Bundesbank; but I noticed that other people eyed him with speculative calculation, not unmixed with sympathy, as you might eye a friend displaying the first dim signs of lunacy, or about to be shut in a cage for a contest with half-starved tigers.

It is all too soon for comfort. Ethiopia is still a long, long way from Huddersfield, and what is happening there is rather like the introduction of proportional representation to some turreted barony of antiquity, all clanking men-at-arms and damsels. But as distasteful and maddening as the process is, even in Ethiopia the World Bank has no choice. If the momentum of change is not maintained, a whole generation will go sour. Already, because the pressure of political enlightenment demands more security for the Throne, schools have actually been closed down to save money for guns: many more such backslidings, political, social, or economic, could lead to catastrophe. At best, Ethiopia might go Communist, as her young intellectuals turn to the political philosophy that seems to offer the speediest prospect of change. At worst, this ancient State, addled by frustration and disillusionment, might degenerate into squalid and fissiparous anarchy, faction against faction, province against province, civil against military, as Shakespeare's violent noblemen squabbled long ago. The Huddersfield road has turnings, Heaven knows, not to speak of potholes and obstructions; but it is, for all its weary travelers, unmistakably a one-way street.

It is only our tumultuous age that has posed these problems of timing and synchronization. Even thirty years ago it would have been unthinkable for a nation in Ethiopia's condition to talk of industrialization. Let me offer you two minor but pungent illustrations. In the 1870's, when Japan was just taking the industrial plunge, Japanese economists had already devised (to give you a taste of their powers even then) a formula concerning tenant-cultivated land that read as follows: L equals $\frac{rRP-(t+t')L}{i}$ where L stands for land value, R for the quantity of rice crop, P for the unit price of rice, r for the percentage of rent to be paid in kind by tenants, t for the rate of land tax, t' for the rate of local surtax, and i for the conversion rate of interest. Nearly a century later, there is scarcely a single Ethiopian capable of producing such a mathematical proposition, and probably not more than a couple of thousand able to understand it.

My second illustration is less esoteric. It took some nine centuries of consistent national development for the British to reach the moment of their mechanical revolution, and even before their emergence as a people they had benefited from a foreign tutelage so advanced that to this day few States in Africa can compare with Roman Britain for order, inventiveness, and logical government. If you visit Nelson's flagship *Victory*, in permanent dry dock at Portsmouth, you may see

The Road to Huddersfield:

a log book kept privately by a midshipman on board the ship in the last decades of the eighteenth century, in the very years of Huddersfield's emergence. He was ten or eleven years old, and was only one of a thousand such boys on board His Majesty's ships of the line. Yet he kept that journal with a painstaking care and accuracy, an attention to detail, a maturity of judgment, a rationality of choice that could scarcely be emulated today, I fear, by more than a few hundred grown men in the whole Empire of Ethiopia. He was not, I suspect, a very interesting lad. He came to nothing. He led no fleets to victory, nor is his writing instinct with much imagination or delicacy of feeling. I have no doubt that in brain-power he would be outclassed by multitudes of clever young Ethiopians. But every page of his book expresses the frame of mind that a nation needs to enter the technical era, just as that Japanese formula demonstrates the caliber of skill that is demanded. The desperate shortage of both in the highlands of Shoah or the Harar market place is a measure of the challenge that such a nation as Ethiopia offers, at such an uncompromising moment of time as ours.

⸴ 4 ⸴

*Yanhee ⸴ the lotus country ⸴
readier than most ⸴ why? ⸴
impulses to change ⸴ in the dam's gift ⸴
doubts ⸴ pains to come ⸴
"a pity"*

HIGH on the Ping River in Siam, any day of the Buddhist year, the traveler wandering upstream may discover one of the bravest spectacles of the contemporary East. The Burmese frontier runs thirty or forty miles to the west, the tangled States of Indochina lie brooding or quarreling to the east, China herself is only a few minutes in an elderly airplane to the north, and in the upper reaches of the valley that waters the whole heartland of Siam, a scoop of watery green among the hills, there stands the Yanhee Dam, a new prodigy of Asia.

It looks noble to anyone, but best of all to the unprepared stranger. South of Yanhee the river winds through its wooded gorge swift but brownish, littered with sandy shallows, stranded branches, and the wicker traps of fishermen. Only a few topsy-turvy villages line its green banks, only a curious bird or two clicks, whistles, or makes a noise out of its tiny belly like the uncorking of a champagne bottle. Crickets chafe and fish jump, and in the forest, I suppose, the leopards are padding, the parrots screeching, the teak-wallah elephants laboring

The Road to Huddersfield:

at their logs. There is a dry scented smell in the air, like the smell inside a tea can. A drum beat emerges sometimes from some buried hamlet in the woods, or a peal of the inescapable Siamese laughter: but mostly the Ping River slides down toward Bangkok silent and purposeful, not unlike a stream of lava. It is mostly wilderness around you, and in the scrubby mountains high above the river gorge, almost nobody lives.

But suddenly you reach Yanhee, and instantly the still is shattered. Suddenly there is movement all about you, and long, low buildings sliding by, like the houses of Memphis or Cairo greeting Huck Finn and Jim on another river far away. Long boats with outboard motors chug to and fro, and jeeps bounce along the foreshore. Music echoes raucously from an outdoor movie. There is a flash of oxyacetyline in a shed, the clang of somebody's hammer, the rumble of a heavy truck. The sweet tea smell has gone, and instead there is a suggestion of oil in the air. A long steady hum of engines reaches you, and as you swing around the last shrub-covered promontory, there before you stands the dam itself, huge, white, and serene. Around it the wooded hills tumble down, thick with brambles, as tangled and untrodden as they have always been: but below them, gleaming there and humming, Yanhee stands like a very talisman of change, a miraculous intrusion, as though its engineers have flown down from Mars itself and brought their anvils with them.

There are some engineering works that can—in theory, anyway—themselves transform the destinies of a nation: in one cutting of the tape, one press of the generating button. The High Dam at Aswan is one: by interrupting the whole antique

The World Bank, Washington

Halifax, Yorkshire

Ethiopian Village

Sukkar Barrage, Indus River, Pakistan

Cefalu, Sicily

Siam: A floating market on one of the crowded Bangkok canals

Atlantic Railroad, Colombia

cycle of flood, fertility, and decay, it offers a dim possibility of catching up at last with the terrifying Egyptian birth rate, and enabling the Nile peoples to think in terms of growth rather than of hectic stagnancy. Another such monumental project is Kariba, the tremendous Zambesi dam that can multiply the potential of the Rhodesias, if politics do not switch its turbines off and drain away its kilowatts. And a possible third is Yanhee, to which the World Bank has, not without its habitual doubts and reservations, contributed a loan of many million dollars. Why this should be, why Yanhee is thought to be necessary, and by what course the gentle Siamese are advancing toward Huddersfield, we shall now, to a tinkle of temple bells and a soft fragrance of joss sticks, hopefully proceed to inquire.

No two countries could be more different than Ethiopia and Siam. They have only three things in common: both are fundamentally prosperous; both are proud and long-lived monarchies; and both sustained their national identities when all around them lofty States toppled one by one into the maw of empire. In all other respects they are as different as a phoenix from an anteater, and it is no surprise to discover that though the Siamese maintain diplomatic missions in Saudi Arabia, Norway, and New Zealand, not to mention a Royal Thai Consulate in Miami, they remain unrepresented in Addis Ababa.

If the Ethiopians so far have few of the skills necessary to the technical revolution, the Siamese give you the impression that if they really wanted to, they could easily split the atom or send a rocket into outer space. They are a most

The Road to Huddersfield:

capable and cultivated people, who have been studying the ways and outlooks of the West at least since the days of Anna Leonowens, and who have succeeded perhaps better than any other people in fusing the occidental and the oriental styles without tarnish or disgruntlement. They leave you with no sour taste in the mouth, no sense of impending dismay, for there is something about them that discourages anxious speculation and calms all our forebodings. Nowadays the modernists call their country Thailand, an unmusical bastard name, but Siam suits her much better; for she is an elegant, sinuous, sibilant sort of State, like a gilded snake on a slim wrist, or one of those enchanting mythical creatures, part bird, part beast, part maiden, who stand guard down the ages over her own Buddhist temples. In Siam it is exceedingly difficult to concentrate upon the progress of the world, for there is always a laugh in the room next door, always a gurgle of the river outside, always a fragile light-footed servant to bring you your aromatic fish, and even the laundry lists of the Bangkok hotels divert you from serious meditation by quoting prices for laundering either your turban or your watch band. The very notion of economics seems an irrelevance, such a lotus country is Siam.

This is not only escapism. The elusive nature of Siamese affairs is one of the national facts. Here pleasure really is *blunter* than duty. Politics in Siam are not at all intrusive, not at all cut and dried, and they do not often intrude into everyday conversation. The average Siamese is scarcely a political animal, and the nation tiptoes down the decades, ever graceful, ever amusing, as though it is independent of governments, alliances, development schemes and all, and is only rehearsing

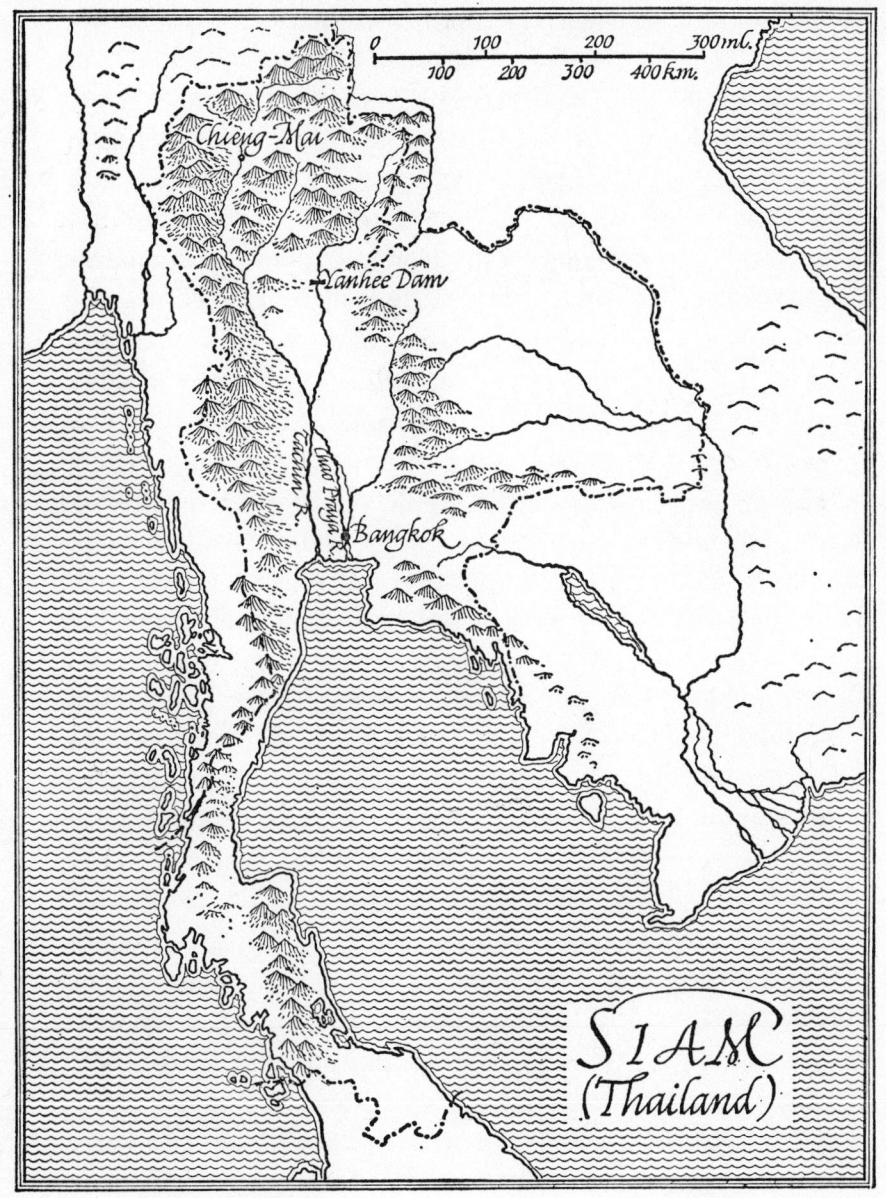

The Road to Huddersfield:

one of the classic maneuvers of the national ballet—The Salutation of the Celestials, perhaps, or The Hare Admires the Moon. Like Ethiopia, Siam is an autocracy, but she hardly trembles to the gauleiter or rings to the midnight knock. In this country unpleasantness seldom goes further than "misunderstanding," as the Siamese like to define their declaration of war against Britain and the United States in 1942, and for most of its citizens it is a genuinely happy place.

A gift for easygoing skepticism greases the cogs of Siamese life. This is partly the fortunate product of independence. It is partly climatic: Siam lies in a comfortable mean between the sweaty and the shivery. It is partly native temperament and ability: the Siamese are not only invigorated by the millions of Chinese immigrants within their frontiers, but are also Chinese by derivation themselves, and retain, if not the grandeur, at least some of the quick initiative of their majestic origins. In the anxious context of Southeast Asia, Siam feels a sort of haven, where there is food enough for nearly all, where a bloody revolution seems almost unthinkable, where there is no froward jockeying between the cultures and no harsh conflict between the ancient and the innovating. Nowhere in Siam is so primitive as Gondar, and nobody is half so grand as Haile Selassie.

Siam is fortified by a colorful monarchy and a magnificent religion, and traditions of charming continuity run through every strand of her society. Never was there a grander water spectacle than the annual royal visit to the temple called Wat Arun, when the King and Queen of Siam, gorgeously caparisoned in gold, are rowed down the Bangkok river in barges of dreamlike fancy, with swans' heads for prows and many-headed serpents all around the poop. Nowhere is there a more exhilarating building than the temple of the Emerald Buddha in Bangkok, a miracle of color and vivacity, guarded by huge demon sentinels, populated by stone cows and marble elephants, giants, bronze lions couchant, colored monkeys, thrown together with such proliferation of fancy, frequented by such gay throngs of country visitors, touched so delicately by a glint of sun, a whisper of leaves, and a soft clinking of bells, so instinct with a spirit of gay and unpretentious reverence that when you walk through its outer gate and see its little world of wonders before you, all you can do is lean against a pillar and laugh aloud with delight.

Siam is full of inherited honorifics, patronymics, and royal laterals, arranged in such elaborate orders of heredity that a title diminishes in value generation by generation, from splendor to dignity, from dignity to pride, from pride to obscurity, until in the end it fades away altogether, like the face of the Cheshire Cat, leaving only an amused smile in the family mansion. Siam is graced and ennobled by Buddhism—a religion still in its prime, still so compelling that most young men of this kingdom, for three months of their lives, put on the saffron robes and submit to the 227 rules of monastic discipline. Everywhere there are temples: here a shrine shaped like a Chinese junk, here one fortified with crumbling watchtowers, here one built over a bone from the Lord Buddha's skeleton, here one dedicated to the art of meditation, where you may watch the aspirants practicing the correct rhythms of contemplative walk. Everywhere there are the tokens of sovereignty, from flood-lit equestrian monuments to the Grand Palace of the Thai kings. This palace, a mile square, is won-

The Road to Huddersfield:

derfully spectacular, with its attendant temples and its gilded effigies, its City of Forbidden Women, its high fretted walls like an eastern Kremlin, its snake eaves and its steep-pitched roofs, its throne halls and elaborate shuttered drawing rooms. Siam remains, for all her westernization, overwhelmingly Siamese. She is mistress of her own land, her own culture, her own language, her own fleets and armies, her own exchequer, her own alphabet (not quite so florid as Amharic, but still boasting thirty-two vowels and forty-four consonants). She is, as nearly everyone agrees, one of the very sweetest of kingdoms, and she is also one of the luckiest.

She lies in the cockpit of Southeast Asia, and in that welter of confused loyalties, unpronouncable names, and indistinguishable politicians, she feels enviably assured. She is tucked snugly away at the head of her own gulf, temptingly stocked with foodstuffs and resources: tin, teak, rubber, and rice so abundant that day and night her barges chug down to the sea loaded deep with sustenance for less fortunate peoples. She is like a well-stocked store in a shabby suburb: rich herself, and spacious, but surrounded by Powers of crowded discomfiture. She is built, so to speak, around a river—the Chao Phraya, which means "Senior Lord" (one of whose tributaries, far up toward China, is the Ping). With this great stream as her spine, and a mesh of rivulets and canals as her ribs, she is quintessentially green, lush, and fecund. She is a water-State. The plain that runs southward to Bangkok is one long sweep of paddy fields, through which the gray water buffaloes, tick birds imperturbable upon their shoulders, stalk their soggy way with aloof solemnity. Grandly through Bangkok itself strides the great river, alive with sampans, ferry boats, daintily fringed tourist launches, rafts of teak from the upland forests, deep-sea ships from the China Sea, slender gray warships, and Edwardian tugs. In the country around the capital thousands of water people live in the damp woods, their houses on stilts at the water's edge, their temples strangled with opulent foliage, their children born to boats and mud pies, their morning markets assembled in flotillas of canoes, with the housewives paddling calmly about beneath their enormous circular straw hats, like so many elegant marsh insects out of the rushes.

This is a country blessed always with warmth and palm thatch, fertile sometimes almost to obscenity, and so rich in nutriment that after a heavy rain you occasionally find edible fish splashing about in the puddles. Step off at any riverside hamlet below Yanhee and you will detect at once the presence of *baraka*—an abstraction the Arabs coined to describe the condition of being both blessed in a passive sense and benevolent in an active. On a hump among the houses stands the temple, a solitary young priest thoughtful in fluttered saffron at its gate, and below this fulcrum of spiritual guidance the village lies idle but content. Nowhere are there signs of want. The houses are charmingly and substantially built of teak, and the little shops are full of good things—succulent vegetables, buckets of eels and prawns, stinking trays of dried fish, baskets of squashy fruit. A myriad entrancing babies look out sleepily from their hammocks; a hundred dormant citizens, flat on their backs in the sunshine, open one eye and offer you a passing twinkle; in the children's playground a dozen unmistakable cherubs, demurely cross-legged in the grass, are chattering like chipmunks around a game of leap-frog. It is true that the indolence of such a village is partly the torpor of disease, but if there is anyplace in the world where the old pastoral way can still keep a people happy, it is in these rich rice lands of Siam. Nobody starves in such a village. Nobody is really hungry. The very jungle all around is full of sweet potatoes, edible lizards, queer prickly fruits that are only waiting to be plucked, skinned, and gobbled. The philosophy of this land is kindly and easygoing, and the divine response has been distinctly favorable.

For a central glimpse of this Siamese euphoria, so rare a quality in our star-crossed generation, let me take you to the shrine of the civic soul in Bangkok, the very ark of Siam's covenant with life. Most cities have a soul of sorts, of course, but it is characteristic of this country that Bangkok's should be publicly on display, for all to see, enjoy, and supplicate. Out of this little shrine, which stands almost opposite the Grand Palace, a kind of sensual haze seems always to emanate, drifting idly across the neighboring rooftops and disarming all instincts of quibble or disdain. The courtyard of the place is always full of people: mendicants selling caged birds to be released "for merit," peddlers touting lucky charms, horoscopes, or green sweetmeats, platoons of bright-eyed children and blithe old crones, and perhaps a sozzled beggar to wring your heart with a celestial grin. At the back of the yard, to the clash of cymbals and the wheezing of an oboe, three or four mature dancing girls are always performing the stylized evolutions of a dance-drama. Here is the elephant, holding her tusks precariously on her head and moving in a heavy highfooted prance; and here is the hero, a buxom forty, heavily rouged and flourishing a sword with vim; and there beside the stage is the band, squatting on the floor with its strange beguiling instruments, tinkling and thudding and bumping and gasping, and sometimes winking at you through the counterpoint. A pungent smell of curry hangs upon the air, and always above the hubbub flows the hollow liquid music, like an odd but merry plain chant.

And in the middle of it all, neon-lit in an alcove, stands the sacred pillar itself, the soul of a city. Before it stands a table of offerings—a pig's head on a platter, an egg upon a dish, a bowl of petals, a vase of sweet-smelling leaves. Around it the citizenry lovingly moves, kneeling with prayer rattles, burning joss sticks, arranging flowers, whispering, praying, or just staring. There is nothing creepy, ominous, or forbidding about the sanctuary. It feels the happiest and friendliest of oracles, and as you stand there in the half-light with a joss stick in your hand, in a trice you find you have succumbed to the inspiration of the place yourself, and feel a voluptuous sort of virtue entering your veins.

This is the country that the Yanhee dam, with a rumble of its Japanese turbines, is destined to electrify.

Why? Well, first of all, why not? This is no Ethiopia, retarded in isolation and temperamentally unready for the great change. The Siamese are readier than most. They are an easygoing people, but they well understand the advantages of commerce and industry. The Chinese community, in particular, mastered the techniques of the investor and the entrepreneur long ago: drive into any up-country village in Siam, and there in the main street you will find, like a blazing island of capitalism, the Chinese restaurant, fragrant with the delicate spices,

The Road to Huddersfield:

herbs, and sauces of a noble cuisine—more than a restaurant, too, a sort of generator, for its proprietor is probably moneylender as well, banker very likely, marriage broker sometimes, hotelier if anyone asks, informant to every stranger, confidant to every official. Whenever the people of Siam extract themselves from the fragrant ease of their lovely civilization, they prove themselves able merchants and administrators. They have an old tradition of scholarship and education. Many a Siamese economist could devise an accurate correlation of local surtax and conversion rates of interest, and the midshipmen of the Royal Siamese Navy I'm sure would perfectly satisfy Lord Nelson. An American economic mission, visiting Siam a year or two ago, pronounced her the most promising of all Asian countries for foreign investment. She knows the language of profit, and you have only to look at the burgeoning skyline of Bangkok, the towering new hotels and the bright new office blocks, to see how effectively she has established her credit among the financiers. The World Bank has made seven separate loans to the Siamese, and seems to have not the slightest doubt that they will be repaid.

Siam has stability, that prerequisite of technical revolution. It is a stability temperamental, emotional, and religious, fostered by deep national pride, resilient tradition, and the calm benignity of Buddhism. If you considered only the newspaper clippings you might think her something less than even-keeled, for her recent history has been a fusillade of coups, countercoups, erupting despots, and stifled grandees, and her present political regime is so rigidly autocratic that the officially nominated National Assembly includes fifty-nine generals, ten admirals, and a clutch of air marshals. But this is normal enough in Siam. It is accepted without much concern, and though the country always buzzes with rumors of mayhem and political skulduggery, though official life is riddled with nepotism and venality, though the succession of one premier to another is fraught always with possibilities of violence, nevertheless the continuity of the State does not often feel threatened. A change of regime does not much upset the rhythm of Siamese life. As one official publication disarmingly observes, "such disturbances have no effect on the peace of the country and on the continuity of policy as framed by the patriotic officers of the Army, Navy and Police forces." It is perfectly true. Siam is an autocracy, but an autocracy of calculated benevolence, mild enough to keep the populace content, alert enough to keep it disciplined.

The youngbloods of Siam, the potential men of Huddersfield, do not seem to be in the mood of *saevo indignatio* which we felt so vividly in Ethiopia and which almost alone is propelling that strange comity toward modernism. If you stay clear of politics, after all, life in Siam can be almost narcotically agreeable. There is a lull to the very air of the place, the creaking of the tall teak forests, the lapping of the canals, the gentle swaying of the little kingfishers who sit like neat blue idols on almost every telegraph wire. A place like Chieng-Mai, the old walled Chinese town in the north of Siam, seems positively paved with languorous satisfaction: the fluffy dogs are patted and pampered, the wrinkled old men are wreathed in smiles, and even the beggar boys at the pavement café, crinkling up their foreheads and whining their high-pitched appeals—even those sorry urchins, when you are goaded into slipping them

The Road to Huddersfield:

a coin or two, turn out to be doing it, as you suspected, only for a lark.

In such a social climate, educated frustration has not yet appeared: partly because education is rooted and widespread, partly because of Buddhism's tolerant consolations, partly because, in a country of old culture and sophistication, educated men do not have much to be frustrated about. Among nations as among people, the more highly civilized you are, the less obsessed with material advance, the more willing you are to live quietly beside a duck pond. It is no coincidence that Burma, that gilded stronghold of Buddhism, is perhaps the only country on earth that shows no eagerness at all to take the Huddersfield road. There are few furious adolescents in Siam. Sometimes young hackles may rise against the pretensions of Siamese royalty: it is the custom that nobody may stand higher than the seated King, and this palace protocol sometimes irks those citizens who do not much like crawling around the floor before their monarch in tight skirts and stiletto heels. Sometimes a resolute idealist protests, for a month or two, against the old habits of Siamese corruption, or the ostentation of the current dictator. Such moments of indignation do not usually last long, though; for the most part, Siamese of all classes are happy—not quite so happy as the travel writers would have you think, but still blithe enough. Sometimes the laughing, gentle effervescence of Siamese life seems to mask some inner emptiness or uncertainty; but a country with such gnarled loyalties and instincts does not easily fall into anarchy or despair, for all its permutations of political fortune.

Thus, to the investigators of the World Bank, Siam seems to be, as the estate agents speciously say, ripe for development.

In many respects she seems to stand at the very gates of Huddersfield. She has the ability to industrialize, the stability, the financial comprehension, the convenient veneer of westernization. She has an able educated class, a prosperous economy, plenty of room, and not too many people. In some ways she is quite advanced already: in 1958 well over half her towns and villages had electricity, compared with 2.7% in India. The only thing she seems to lack, just at the moment, is the national will to change. Many an eager Siamese hopes to make his fortune out of industry; but many more are not terribly interested in the miracles of science, far prefer the country to the town, and are content to continue in the old style, watching the moon rise above the temple eaves, and singing quaint songs to eccentric rhythms.

So why? Is it necessary to transform this delightful country? Will the Siamese be happier when the dams and the mills go up, the speed of life is intensified, every man has a car in his garage and a transistor blaring in his pocket? Is the World Bank justified in hastening the technical revolution in such a State, regardless of all that will go by the computer board? Does not everybody sometimes feel that some old important magic is squeezed out of life by the machine and its acolytes, some deeper human fulfillment? For myself, I cannot help loathing the prospect of an industrial Siam, and I very much doubt if this people will be happier in a century's time than it is now: but, all the same, you can well see how many and how insidious are the pressures that impel a society toward change, and how impossible they are to resist.

As always, nationalism is one such impulse—sometimes con-

The Road to Huddersfield:

scious and tub-thumping, sometimes nagging away beneath the body politic like a pulse in the blood. It has been said that every technical revolution, from Huddersfield on, has been sparked by some sense of national slight or isolation: in Britain, the very fact of insular survival; in Russia, a century of humiliations, from Napoleon to the Russo-Japanese war; in China, the long, slow nibblings of the foreign barbarians; in Japan, the sudden cataclysmic revelation of Perry's squadron after two centuries of segregated inbreeding. Siam, too, is subject to such proddings of testy nationalism, not because she has been debased, but because she stands all alone among her neighbors.

In Southeast Asia she is the sole champion of the western way, the capitalist way, which may help to account for the enthusiasm of that American mission. Around her the Burmese, the Laotians, the Cambodians, the Malayans, and the Chinese are at best neutral in the conflict between the ideologies, at worst deeply suspicious of everything western; but in Siam, for all the dazzling exotica, you are unmistakably within the capitalist camp. The hulking transports of the United States Air Force are always at Bangkok airport, the hum of western strategy infuses the capital, and all the agencies of the western alliance, from educational teams to helicopter pilots, swarm through this kingdom in ceaseless proliferation. All the paraphernalia of the western way has fallen upon Siam —club sandwich and Rotary Club, pop singers and paper-back poets—and this has set her apart among her peers, put her warily on guard, and pricked her rather waspishly toward Huddersfield.

She too is a kind of island. She marches with four varied

nations—to the south Malaya, to the west Burma, to the east Laos and Cambodia—but her own frontiers are well defined, and she presents a trim, orderly impression of symmetry and completeness, a water garden fenced by hills. Among her neighbors she is not very popular. The Cambodians distrust her so intensely that the two countries, glaring at each other across an often debated frontier, no longer indulge in diplomatic relations. (One of the more colorful of the cases recently heard by the International Court at The Hague was that concerned with the disputed possession of a Khmer temple on the border between these quarrelsome kingdoms.) The Malayans have not forgotten that during World War II the Siamese accepted substantial chunks of Malayan territory from their Japanese allies. The Laotians are always afraid that one day the Siamese, with American support, will take over their various regions in the name of democratic preventive security. The atmosphere of Siam is altogether seductive, as alluring as the flowers of her ornamental pools, but the local reputation of this State is something less than fragrant. She is alienated from her hinterland, and this faint suggestion of the lovely pariah itself constitutes a historical impulse toward progress.

There are less metaphysical urges, too, notably the existence of one depressed and relatively impoverished province within these fruitful frontiers. If you drive eastward from the rice fields of the Chao Phraya, you cross a low, dour, rather dingy ridge of hills pierced by a solitary highway. The moment you are over this insignificant divide, you feel yourself in a different land. Gone is the well-fed idle charm of the Ping villages, or the gay gusto of Bangkok. Half gone is the sensation of

The Road to Huddersfield:

endless carefree courtesy, the *dolce far niente* that soothes the vexations of this country and keeps the hedonist ever satisfied. The northeast of Siam is a grimmer, harsher place. Even here, I am assured, nobody is starving, though some very primitive peoples indeed swing among the forest trees: but in this dry and bony terrain there is a shortage of that Asiatic staple, rice, without which every Siamese feels himself to be undernourished. A friend of mine once asked a citizen of the northeast how long he could keep himself alive in the jungle with his gun. "Ten days," was the answer. "After that I'd die of malaria." "Yes, yes," my friend said, "but assuming you'd been immunized against malaria: how long then?" "Three weeks," that lugubrious rustic replied. "After that I'd die for lack of rice."

He wouldn't, of course, for he could live comfortably enough on wild strawberries, fungi, and stewed snakes, but his prognosis well expresses the spirit of deep, sapless dissatisfaction that seems to inform his part of the country. If there is not starvation up there, at least there is proper poverty. There are crippled indigents about, and wizened children, and stooped, whining young mothers. Dissident movements are always busy in the bushes, plotting Communist coups or separatist gestures. Agents filter through from Laos or Communist North Vietnam, even from old China herself (whose very existence is not recognized in Bangkok, where people often tell you of a visit to China but mean they have lately spent a weekend in Taipeh).

Up in the northeast you may sometimes feel the underlying tensions of autocracy in Siam, when you read of another mass arrest or observe a sudden arbitrary reshuffling of regional governors. People are sometimes shot for treason there, and many more, briskly labeled as Communist subversives, are whisked away to places of detention for courses of corrective training. The northeast stands to the rest of Siam as the altiplano, say, stands to the opulent coastline of Peru. Just as the ignorant, embittered, diseased Indians flock out of their mountains to squat in the vile slums around Lima, so the poor folk of the Siamese northeast look with longing toward the fecund river valley, or swarm down to fester in the purlieus of Bangkok. Their province is an awkward brooding skeleton in the Siamese cupboard, always likely to burst open the doors and clatter into the kitchen: raising its living standards, and bringing it into a happier co-operation with the rest of the country, is one urgent and proper reason to industrialize.

And further away still, on an even more remote horizon, looms the ultimate justification. Siam today is plagued with few of the standard Asian problems. In her freedom from terrible physical pressures, she is more like a nation of Africa or South America, where the prospects are boundless, the prairies are illimitable, and there is food and wealth enough for all. Traveling direct to Bangkok from the scabbed huggermugger horrors of Calcutta is like moving out of a nightmare into a rhapsody: the relief is overwhelming, just as the general air of competence and order is invigorating to a degree. Even in this little Paradise, though, it is not going to last. Since 1930 the population has doubled, and it is increasing faster each year as the miracles of medicine reduce the death rate. No wars or dreadful calamities have kept the multiplication of the Siamese in check. The very benevolence of the countryside ensures that their march toward congestion proceeds calmly, in-

The Road to Huddersfield:

exorably, and fast. There are more than 20 million Siamese today: by the end of this century there will probably be 50 million, too many even for this generous countryside to sustain by the old means. Today Siam earns her foreign exchange by the export of rice: then she will need it all for herself, and different indeed will be the flavor of her being—if the 1,000 million Chinese, bursting their own frontiers in search of living room and foodstuffs, have not already swamped her.

Thus we see in Siam a situation diametrically opposed to that in Ethiopia, yet no less unmistakably edging a nation toward technocracy. The Ethiopians scarcely need to change, but angrily want to; the Siamese must, but scarcely feel the urge. The Ethiopians have not yet acquired the basic attitudes and textures of modernity; the Siamese are almost too sophisticated, so serene, unflustered, and cultured is their pattern of life. The Ethiopians are basically rich, and likely to get richer; the Siamese are also prosperous, but are likely to get poorer. The Ethiopians are impelled into change chiefly by politics, by the new insights of education and the frustrations of an antique despotism; the Siamese are half-heartedly on their way to Huddersfield almost because they have no choice, because history, chance, and genetics have conspired to make them a reservation.

The World Bank's contribution to all this has been, as usual, oblique in character. A Bank representative lives permanently in Bangkok, and has his office in the very same palace compound where Anna, the English governess, coached the royal children long ago. Directly opposite the door of his room, across a narrow corridor, there stands, dim-lit and peacefully suggestive, one of the innumerable minor shrines of the Grand Palace. There he is very close indeed to the springs of Siamese power, and there he can exert, at the center of things, the Bank's powerful influence toward financial stability and orthodoxy. A web of customary corruption veils the ministerial offices of the Siamese government, and one of the Bank's aims, here as in Ethiopia, has been to establish a standard of values upon which the national institutions of progress can be based.

In Ethiopia the telecommunications board was the chosen instrument of example; in Siam it is the railways. The lines themselves have been modernized, largely with Japanese equipment. (Changing from steam to diesel will, incidentally, preserve the Siamese forests, for hitherto the locomotives have all been wood burners, and were eating up the timber as fast as the pot-chimney engines of the old America swathed their way through the forests of the West.) No less important is the reorganization of management that has accompanied all this, the new levels of administration that have been, if not achieved, at least envisaged, the removal of the railway services from the cramping, stultifying mesh of chicanery and avarice.

Other money has helped to dredge the estuary of the Chao Phraya, enabling big ships to come up to Bangkok, and to build irrigation works upstream, designed to increase the rice and bean crops, and thus tentatively thumb a nose at the rising population. But, most of all, the Bank has interested itself in Yanhee, that sheer white monument high in the forested interior, where the Ping flows through its narrows southward from Chieng-Mai. I visited this marvelous dam when they were still building it, and never did I feel the future pressing

The Road to Huddersfield:

more insistently upon me, nor hear the beat of the winged chariot so loud behind my back. In those days it was brilliantly illuminated at night, so that the whole valley was diffused with a fierce yellowish glare, like the glow of a great city over the hill, and the dam itself looked cold and eerie, like the façade of some monstrous concrete mausoleum.

All night long it teemed and pulsed with energy. At its foot the big trucks lumbered through the dust, and men in red and yellow helmets clambered out of the floodlights into the ribbed recesses of the thing. In half-built structures, half-dug tunnels, caverns part blinding, part shadowy, a multitude of sinewy Siamese worked with an expressionless kind of energy, their faces dry but glinting, and sometimes you would hear a snatch of oriental song or the chatter of Texan voices, strong, loud, and simple. High above the wall of the dam two immense cranes, masterfully silhouetted against the stars, swung and swiveled the small hours away, a fuss of trains, trucks, and laborers around their feet. There was a hissing of steam from a refrigeration plant, and a clatter of railway wagons, and a roaring, and a rushing, and set against the absolute inky silence of the wilderness all about, the brilliance of the Asian stars above our heads, and the dark motion of the river southward toward the sea. Sunk in a chasm in that empty place, the fire and flame of Yanhee seemed to me like a portent of all that Siam must undergo as she painfully eases out of one era into another.

For this great work, set in motion by the men of 1818 H Street, on the other side of the world, can provide the power for the Siamese technical revolution. In that distant kingdom Huddersfield waits upon Yanhee, and Yanhee can do for Siam what the puffing steam engines, water mills, and traction engines did for England 150 years ago—shove this society into the machine age. It is only in our time that one engineering work can so transform a nation, and it is frightening to consider how much hangs in the gift of this dam and thus of the World Bank itself—how many changed lives, how many eager aspirations, how many shattered hopes and disillusionments. The purpose of Yanhee is partly to control floods and partly to increase irrigation, but mostly to provide energy: in the end it can increase by five times the presently installed electrical capacity of the whole kingdom, and thus in one boost propel this Arcady from happy continence to ulcered automation. Such are the responsibilities of H Street, and such is the vehemence of contemporary change, whose pursuit is the inalienable right of human beings everywhere, and which is identified by all the best-informed optimists as being synonymous with progress.

Do I sound doubtful? I am not alone, for there are people in the Bank itself who think the money could better be spent on simple irrigation. But I am thinking of Japan again, the one Asiatic Power that industrialized itself in the nineteenth century. Like Siam, she has inherited a gracious and ancient culture of her own, governed by strict rules of conduct and propriety and offering moral and even esthetic guidance through most of the basic human predicaments. She took the Huddersfield road with such intelligence and such determination that in less than fifty years she transformed herself from archaic traditionalism to become one of the leading military and industrial Powers of the world: yet to this day she has never recovered her old equilibrium or quite learned how to reconcile the old ways with the new. Nobody is gentler or more courteous than the Japanese at home, among the grass screens and exquisite novelties of his own civilization; but no commuters on earth are more brusquely, indeed violently, packed into their trains than the office workers of Tokyo. Nothing is more aristocratically elegant than a Japanese Zen garden, with all its spare scholarly precision, its handful of white pebbles, its impeccably raked sand; but few night clubs are more hideously vulgar than the honky-tonks of the Japanese cities, with their ugly half-westernized youths and their coarsely painted courtesans. Japan is one of the most brilliant of nations, but nobody could call her serene. She is nostalgic still for her own culture, as she plunges ever more giddily, ever more successfully into ours.

Soon Siam too will face these same exigencies. Her period of transition is sure to be painful, sure to be unsightly, and its psychological impact will affect almost all her citizens. Perhaps, though, it will not last so long, now that the world moves faster and people grow up more quickly, forget sooner, and learn more readily. Even in the mellow West the pace of science is astonishing to observe, but we have learned to keep in time with it. Only fifty years ago a Harvard hopeful was asked by his professor to define the nature of electricity. He hummed and hawed for a moment, for he was not a diligent scholar, and then remarked that he *had* known the answer but had unfortunately quite forgotten it. "A pity," said the professor with a donnish sigh. "Only two persons have ever known what electricity is—the Author of Nature and yourself. Now, you say, one of the two has *forgotten.*"

5

*Improper conduct, the two Italies,
the Cassa,
reputation of the south,
obstacles to progress, on the move,
Scopello*

ONE FINE Sardinian summer night I followed a couple of girls up the hill to their home in Cagliari. It is hardly proper, I know, to follow strange girls about the streets, least of all in the service of the International Bank for Reconstruction and Development. But alas, my motives were starkly professional, for I merely wanted to experience with them, in the interests of historical enlightenment, their nightly transition from the future to the past.

Cagliari, the capital of Sardinia, is a boisterous and full-blooded old seaport, scarred and toughened by centuries of rumbustious history. She has been ruled in her time by Arabs and Byzantines, Vandals and Romans, Carthaginians and shadowy Phoenicians, the Dukes of Savoy and the Kings of Aragon, Spanish viceroys and Austrian marshals. There is therefore nothing drab or dowdy about her waterfront, which has seen so many seafarers come and go and is a splendidly racy fusion of styles, with olive skins and palm trees and lean gray warships at their moorings, half European, half Oriental, and all alive with a laughing pride. It was here, in the

The Road to Huddersfield:

via Roma, that I first caught sight of my girls, tidying their back hair on the sidewalk.

They were exquisitely dressed, though not expensively, with a delicacy of taste, a fastidiousness of grooming, a gaiety of step, and an air of decorous but still seductive bubble that would do credit to the smartest Fifth Avenue secretary or rue de Rivoli *midinette*. All around them was a zing of Mediterranean vivacity. Sailors winked at them, students whistled, friends giggled as they passed. The cafés, spilling out across the pavements under the street lights, were properly crowded and animated. Succulent vapors emerged from the restaurants. Squadrons of Fiats scurried up and down the boulevards, and a blaze of lights shone from a destroyer in the harbor. It would make almost any main street seem torpid by comparison, but through it all, my girls sauntered with an easy aplomb, here greeting an acquaintance, there gently rebuffing an electrician's mate first class, now stopping for a fizzy lemonade, now gazing at a shop window, until before long they were picked up in earnest and whisked into an intimate corner of a coffee house, where they spent the rest of the evening in a hedonism so utterly innocuous that their contemporaries in Stockholm or Los Angeles would loftily dismiss it as a waste of talents.

But then, not very late, while the via Roma was still pulsating with zest and enjoyment, those girls bade their admirers a fairly protracted good night and began the long walk home through the centuries. They left the illuminated warships and the sailors' badinage; they took a long last look at the swimsuits in the corner store; they ignored a last solitary student, singing a sickly song to himself in the Largo Carlo Felice;

and, passing through a great gate tower, guarded through the darkness by a sculpted elephant, they returned to the mazy dim-lit quarter of the city called Castello. Instantly modern Europe seemed far away, and all was intricately eastern, with a sandy breath of Africa on the air. Instantly, in that dark jumble of alleys, tunnels, and cramped courtyards, you felt the pressure of poverty all around you, and the secret hiss of superstition. It was a place for beggars and bandy legs, dwarfs, shibboleths, and old wives' tales. The fringes of Castello, beneath their antique ramparts, felt padded and mellow enough, like a marine Jerusalem, but its innermost recesses, as I trailed those girls through the evening, was filled with babble—the rasping of crones, the wailing of cross children, the sibilance of gossips, the tinny singing of shop girls, radios, televisions, raucous laughter, quarrels, and sometimes the deafening shatter of a motorcycle skidding and leaping exuberantly like a dolphin through the labyrinth. Castello is not exactly a slum, I suppose, but it is like a town out of another age, built in an era when ordinary folk could not expect privacy, space, or comfort but lived cheek-by-jowl as a matter of course.

Into this place, with at least a metaphorical sigh, those two girls returned, their footsteps growing ever slower and more laggardly, I imagined, the further they went. They crossed the Piazza Palazzo, with a policeman dreaming outside the Governor's palace, and passed the old cathedral, candlelight still flickering in its windows, and plunged at last into the dark conundrum of their native alley. A scraggy cat was gnawing an intestine outside their door. A baby was screaming for clean diapers down the road. Their mother scolded them

The Road to Huddersfield:

acidly from the back quarters, and their married sister looked them up and down, with all the maddening patronage of experience, I fear. There was a smell of cooking fat, sweat, cats, tobacco, damp stone, and old ladies. There was a hint of bad drainage and a hover of black-skirted aunts.

The girls took their shoes off, reassured their mother with a kiss and a chide, and returned to—where shall I place them?—the sixteenth century, say.

Poverty, ignorance, and disease are not confined to tropic or wasteland. Every great city has its slum, and, like Siam, many a fortunate country possesses its region of depression, left behind by the national momentum and surviving still as a sad anachronism in the age of affluence. The American South was such a region until it achieved its own industrial revolution in the years after the last war. You have only to visit some hamlet in the Tennessee backwoods, with its peeling wooden houses and its racial sourness, the thump of the piano from its Church of God With Signs Following After, the tickle of its dust and the perfume of its magnolia, to realize that even today such a place is still only emerging from primitivism. Once a year at the English village of Worminghall they hold a tug-of-war across the River Thame, and when, in that dank, reedy countryside, you see the losing team pulled inch by inch into the mud, and watch the hilarious ancient faces of the villagers all around, suddenly you know how alive are the old atavistic impulses still, in the heart of the Welfare State. Dublin is as cultivated a city as you will find in Europe, a place born to urbanity and wit, but only an hour's drive to the south you may find communities not unrecognizably

A Journey to Five Continents

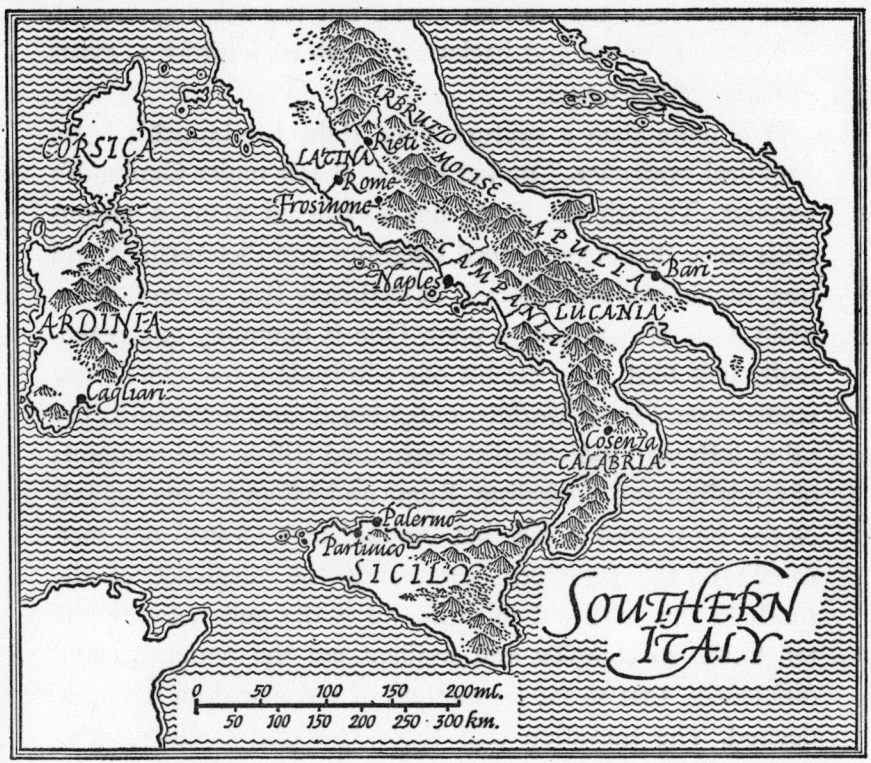

different from the holy island of Berghida. Rio, that benediction among places, commands a hinterland that is half barbarous. Greece, that crucible of our civilization, contains areas not so far removed from animism and banditry (the only inn in Canea, recorded dear old Murray's *Handbook* just seventy years ago, was the Hotel de Rhadamanthe, and the book added by way of impartial assessment: "A dirty hole, not fit for any English traveller"). Most remarkable of all, within sixty miles of Rome, the eternal capital, you may stumble into the Italian south, the Mezzogiorno. Italy has the third largest gold reserves in the western world, but the Mezzogiorno remains as crumbled and backward a slab of territory as exists in democratic Europe.

It is more than a century since Italy, Metternich's "geographical expression," united herself at last under Garibaldi's banners. Though the State has weathered many a vicious crisis since then, experienced kingships and dictatorships and now republican presidencies, nevertheless two Italies still remain. One is rich, one is poor. One is booming, one perennially half bust. One excites our admiration, one chiefly our compassion. One is worldly, enlightened, and materialist, the other lofty and individualist, restrained still by the remnants of feudalism and clericalism. Rome and Milan are the capitals of the prosperous north, but Naples, that ravaged old metropolis of the Bourbons, commands the allegiance of the south to this day; and so profound is the gulf between the territories, so complex and resilient are the temperamental differences, that so far no method of reconciliation has been devised. The transition that those two girls experienced as they wandered home through Cagliari is one that any traveler may taste for himself as he probes his way southward through Italy.

The historical causes of the fissure are complex. Southern Italy, the Magna Graecia of the ancients, was by the course of conquest and culture always detached from the north. One looked south and east, toward Africa and the Aegean; the other across the northern mountains, to Germany and France. The southerners have accordingly seldom shared the manners and mores of the northern Italians, just as, nourished upon the warm beakers of the south, they have never been tempered by those drafts and drizzles that have made us windswept heretics what we are. The economic tentacles of the medieval north, with its brokers and entrepreneurs and elaborate banking systems, never penetrated these tawny Virgilian regions. The northern Italian system of communes, with all its civic self-assertion, never reached the south, and organized as the land was in large feudal entities, often under alien rule, the whole ethos of self-government and social responsibility never mellowed the outlook of its people. The Kingdom of the Two Sicilies, which ruled most of the south until the Risorgimento, had style indeed but was centuries behind the social times: every page of Lampedusa's *The Leopard* demonstrates the absolute supremacy of the great Sicilian landlords half a century and more after the emergence of Huddersfield.

And when Garibaldi triumphed in the south, and was welcomed by a Naples so enthusiastic that the very streets were strewn with straw so as to prevent the carriage wheels from disturbing his sleep—when the glory died down, it was found that the unity of Italy, far from resurrecting the south, only retarded it still further. The legal and administrative customs of the north were merely extended southward willy-nilly, to the grave disadvantage of these simpler parts, and the abolition of tariffs meant that the first struggling industries of the south could no longer compete with Milan and Turin. The proud cities of the Mezzogiorno—Naples, Bari, and Palermo—declined into impotent provincialism, and new men from the north took over. The south of Italy, like the American Confederacy, felt itself exploited, patronized, disregarded, and the people of the north came to regard their sallower-skinned

The Road to Huddersfield:

fellow citizens to the south with something precariously approaching color prejudice: "Africa," as the Florentines still sometimes observe, "begins at Naples." The rise of Italian patriotism only made the contrasts worse. When, in the 1860's, the traveling philosopher George Gissing asked in one southern town what was to be seen there, he was told: *"C'e miseria"*—"Just misery."

This mold of history, coupled with climate and environment, malaria and malnutrition, really has made the southern Italian, as any old soldier will confirm, a different man from the northerner—as different as a Carolina sharecropper, say, from a dairy farmer in Maine. Generalizations are always dangerous, and there are astonishing variations of type and character within the south itself, but it is hypocritical to pretend that Italy forms a homogenous racial whole. In the north they now behave more or less like Swiss or Scandinavians—like whole-hog machine-age western Europeans. In the south they still display the characteristics of the traditional stage Italian, with his charm and his apparent indolence, his style and his vanity and even occasionally his greased mustaches. The north is coruscating as never before since the days of the Renaissance. The shape of our cars, the allure of our actresses, the swing of our skirts, the tunes we whistle, the curtains we hang—all stem indirectly as often as not from the reviving genius of Rome, Florence, Milan, and Turin, which has stamped its ideas indelibly upon the taste of the world. The south still yearns for *il honore* more than *la ricchezza*—prestige rather than income, power, respect, and authority. Northern Italy has triumphantly immersed itself in the technical age, and the only reason why the sale of motorcycles is sluggish in Milan is the fact that nearly everybody now has a car. The south is haunted still by older values of ambition and plagued by a squalor and ignorance that can scarcely be matched in western Europe: poverty barefoot, poverty with rickets, poverty illiterate—so cruel that in the province of Basilicata seven babies in every hundred die in infancy; so animal that in many a Sicilian house the cow lives in the very same room as its master and his family. The south has been depressed for twenty centuries: in the sixth century Gregory the Great described the Sardinians as being *sicut insensata animalia*—"like brute beasts."

Thus within one country you may observe the ages side by side, before and after Huddersfield. Ending this harsh Italian dichotomy, removing the south's causes for grievance or despair, is one of the prime political and moral duties of contemporary Europe; for this is a proud, industrious, hot-blooded people, neither isolated like the Ethiopians nor acquiescent like the Siamese, and it well understands what is meant by the illumination of choices. It is proud of its own ways, but inevitably envious of the other half. For fifty years and more, *la problema del Mezzogiorno* has been one of the prime facts of Italian politics, and many commentators have seen in it the seeds of Mussolini's vainglorious but pathetic efforts to make of Italy a Great Power, and thus plaster over the crack in the shape of the nation.

On the face of things the south often seems beyond redemption and repair, for there are simply too many people for its largely unfertile territories. Every year many thousands of its citizens, reaching this very conclusion, pack their bags and emigrate, and most serious commentators now seem to

The Road to Huddersfield:

agree that the south cannot approach equality without a reduction in its population. In the meantime, though, the Republican Government of Italy is making the first determined, co-ordinated, properly planned attempt to improve the conditions of the south, and to this task the World Bank has contributed a good deal of money. The agency of salvation is called *Cassa per il Mezzogiorno*—Fund for the South—and it is claimed to be the only long-term development plan now being implemented in western Europe. It was this great organization that I had in mind as I followed the girls beneath that guardian elephant: for the Cassa intends to sweep away all that Castello represents, all that is old and dirty and outworn and blinkered, all that is curdled and black-skirted in alleyways.

This is a process different in kind from most of the Huddersfield movements, for here, though the territory is backward enough, the central administration is exceedingly advanced. Here there is no problem of management or governmental attitude, no frittering of funds in blatant venality, no rearguard despot in command. The people are capable of change, and the government wants to change them. The Italian Civil Service is among the most bumble-headed in all Europe, but the men who run the Cassa per il Mezzogiorno seem to be a breed apart. The offices of the Fund, in Rome, are palatial but not hothouse. Its methods are in general much admired. Its publications are models of discreet self-congratulation. Its purposes are statutorily defined, and it seems to have few illusions. This is rather like a colonial situation in the most enlightened of empires, except that there is no real danger that the administration is shortly to be swept into limbo and replaced by feathered primitives of ferocious ineptitude. The critics say, of course, that the Cassa's efforts are really engulfed in muddle, waste, and corruption. Though I do not doubt that it is less lily-white than the World Bank fondly likes to suppose, nevertheless I accept the judgment of those, nearer the Italian soil, who declare it to be one of the very best implements of progress the Italians have ever devised.

The Cassa, which is called "an autonomous public body," was established in 1950, and has taken within its ambit eight mainland regions (Latina, Frosinone, Rieti, Abruzzi and Molise, Campania, Apulia, Lucania, and Calabria) plus the islands of Sicily and Sardinia, the two largest in the Mediterranean. Its northernmost territory is thus actually north of Rome, while its southernmost is almost as far south as Algiers. More than a third of the Italians live in these parts, but their average income is less than half the average in the north. Half the population works on the land, compared with a third in the north, and only one in twelve works in industry, compared with one in five in the north (even in Denmark, that paragon of an agricultural society, one man in seven works in a factory). Where there is industry, it is usually minor—a woodwork factory, a repair shop, a canning plant—and, indeed, most people in southern industry work for firms employing less than ten people. Where there is good land, it has often been wrecked by a cruel cycle of flood and drought. Where there have been plans for dams and aqueducts, there has hitherto been no money to pay for them. "*Nobody* travels south of Rome," Norman Douglas was told when he first proposed to visit Calabria; and though the tourists have long

The Road to Huddersfield:

overstepped the limit, to this day it is a dashing northern industrialist who will risk his profits in the south.

All this the Cassa is trying to alter, with the help of seven sizable loans from H Street. It could not succeed were it not for the fact that malaria has been eradicated—a victory commemorated on almost every gatepost by the painted date of the last DDT spray. Malaria has been fundamental to the degradation of the south, and lay behind the southerner's grossly unfair reputation for feckless laziness. Only a mile or two behind the hills of Cagliari, for example, you will enter country that was, until a few years ago, emasculated, desolated, and impoverished by the scourge. Nearly everybody had malaria, and almost every innovation was stymied by its prevalence. The potentially fertile plains were largely uninhabited, for the people had been forced away from the mosquito hollows into the arid mountain regions, where the land was good only for grazing. Doctors, teachers, and administrators hated to be sent to Sardinia. Industry and tourism shunned the island, and it was a great place for prisons, giving it a sad, penitential flavor. In the northern part of Sardinia there is an agricultural settlement which was founded by the Fascists and was originally called Mussolinia. This was an early attempt to bring modern methods to this ravaged region, and it began bravely, with hundreds of stalwart settlers imported from Venetia, and every technical convenience. Slowly it rotted, though, corroded by that atmosphere of sick fatalism; one by one the families went home; brick by brick the houses crumbled; until in the 1940's, I am told, it looked much like any other part of the destitute south, wasted and depressed. Malaria kept this country always bloodless. The hill towns of Calabria and Sicily were built on their high eminences partly for defense against malaria, but chiefly to keep their heads free of noxious vapors ("malarious exhalations," as Baedeker used to call them); and it is a sad paradox of these parts that the best farming land, down in the valleys, was left to the tillage of the weakest and least-determined farmers —those who, through lack of will or excess of fatalism, chose to live among the mosquitoes in the lowlands.

This horrible blight has been lifted at last, and has given the Cassa at least a possibility of success. There are millions of acres of southern land that can now be reclaimed and improved—about a third of the total area of the south. The great feudal estates have mostly been broken up under the Land Reform laws, and the whole agricultural system is now being modernized with new irrigation works, flood controls, technical education, and co-operatives. The first preoccupation of the Cassa has been with agriculture, but at the same time the infrastructure of industry is hopefully being built— roads, railways, power stations, water supplies, sewage—and industry itself is being tempted southward by all kinds of tax and transport concessions. Tourism is being cherished, and public health improved, and schools are belatedly erected, and new villages founded. The Cassa plans to provide proper water supplies for all the 2,600 communities within its bailiwick, only 108 of which enjoyed such conveniences in 1958. It proposes to sponsor more than 300 new hotels. It has restored the Temple of Jupiter Anxur at Terracina, financed some of the new excavations at Pompeii, turned the Capodimonte Museum in Naples into the most beautiful art gallery in Europe. The Cassa has concerned itself with fishing boats

The Road to Huddersfield:

and super-highways, village churches and technical schools, the production of olives and the survival of folk industries.

And not least it has concerned itself with people, for nothing is more resilient than habit, and nothing more stubborn than an old agricultural society, long bullied and scorned, when at last it is free to change its ways. It is like a bull which, having stormed and charged against its fence all afternoon, refuses to go out when the gate is opened. The Cassa describes its efforts to change popular attitudes as "measures capable of directing the great spiritual gifts and the powerful ingenuity of the people of the south toward new tasks." Sometimes, though, even its calm patience seems liable to fray. The old slow conservatism of the agricultural south, I once heard a Cassa official guardedly observe, "demands the greatest political commitment possible within the limits of parliamentary democracy"—by which he meant that if the cows won't go to pasture, they may have to be pushed.

There is no denying the irritations of the south, the miasmic or evasive character that has helped for so many centuries to preserve both its self-respect and its backwardness. Outside Cosenza I once gave a lift to a woman dressed all in black who was clutching a posy of lilies and thus seemed especially deserving of indulgence. Unhappily, I took an instant dislike to her when once she had settled herself, breathing heavily, beside me in the car. I disliked her stertorious pantings, I disliked the slightly musklike scent she wore, I disliked her gloomy black hat and the lilies nodding pendulously in the corner of my eye, and, above all, I disliked a habit she had of constant squirming and writhing motion.

"My brother-in-law," she presently observed, in a tone of voice at once prim, obsequious, and insidiously false, "my brother-in-law, a man of brilliant experience and ability, who speaks four languages with equal fluency, has told me that the English are more honest than the Calabrese. Is this so?" As she said this, I felt rising within me, quite unfairly, all the old prejudices of the north against the south, of logic against passion, of order against emotion, and when she asked me again, looking rather pertly up into my face—"eh, signor, eh, is it true?"—I answered her unkindly. "Perfectly true," said I with a rush, "and, what's more, in England *ladies don't wriggle!*"

I could have bitten my tongue off as soon as I said it, for I knew I was only expressing an instinct shameful and injurious. But ill-manners are all too common, even among travelers normally tolerant and businessmen normally farsighted, when they reach the south of Italy from the north, exchanging the straight eye and the correct change for all the old mesh of Mediterranean persiflage. The compulsions of history, of climate, of religion have molded these southerners into a kind that often annoys us. Nobody can help enjoying or admiring much about the Italian south, from the beauty of a man's posture to the diligence of a peasant's husbandry, but all too often the southerners feel, as we are liable to say with a sniff, not altogether our style. "Africa begins at Naples," and even today there is at least one professor at the University of Cagliari who cannot bring himself to live there but commutes to his lecture room from Florence.

As much as anything it is the legend of organic unreliability, the annoyance of a poor woman's wriggle, that keeps the south of Italy half estranged from the north. Indeed, it is partly justified. The muffled flavor of the south does mask some fearful anachronisms, and it is arguable that my two girls in Cagliari are still less at home down on the via Roma than they are in all the shadowy squalor of their home. The southern Italians still have little idea of labor contracts, land values, economic conventions, and business protocol. Their social conscience is still rudimentary. Scarred from the old brands of feudalism, war, ignorance, and poverty, they are pre-eminently opportunists—with their neighbors, with their visitors, with their employers, even with their God. They are hamstrung still by their environment, and they await almost without knowing it, like inmates in an institution, some liberating force to sweep them off their feet.

The south is not apathetic toward progress, but it is often instinctively obstructive. Here there is no political hurdle to surmount and no narcotic languor to counter: there are no more hard-working people than these, when once they are released from disease. However, in the hearts of many southern Italians, there is a deep-rooted sense of suspicion and prickly resentment, almost a pride in their poverty, a defiant clinging to their own values. In Spain they call this deep, mysterious folk feeling *casticismo*, something that binds all Spaniards to their own traditions and unites them in a manner of thought. In Southern Italy, oddly enough, they sometimes call it *spagnolismo*, because they believe that it sprang from the years of Spanish dominance. Every visitor to Naples comes away rightly shocked by the slums of that noble city: the stony, stinking alleys strung with shirts, the dim, peeling hovels and shacks, the sleepless street corners streaked with urine, where the skinny, wide-eyed children play. Not many native Neapolitans, though, will offer you a complaint, for the character of their city stands beyond poverty or wealth, away in the heady realms of faith, heritage, and tradition. Certainly the citizens are living five to a room, cooking their macaroni in the streets outside, sharing their every snore with a score of neighbors, urged sometimes to thieving and prostitution, ill-fed and unschooled and often sick; but over the centuries they have made a way of life out of it, and have infused their hardships with a curious dignity. They are devoted to their families, to their city, to the lost cause of Italian royalism. With all their bonds of intimacy and comradeship, they sometimes seem almost enviable, and their miseries are tempered always by pride, loyalty, and old emotion.

All over the south this devotion to old orders, whether deliberate or subconscious, is movingly apparent. In Sicily you may often meet men who have made small fortunes in America or Australia but have come home to end their lives in ancestral simplicity—so deep are their loyalties and so entwined their roots. In some parts of Sardinia they still speak a kind of Latin—*cras* means "tomorrow," *domu*, "house," *nemmos*, "nobody"—and so tight-knit are the communities that an ornithologist recently touring those parts found that a wagtail was called by nine different names in nine different neighboring villages. In many a small but lofty southern town, old men in black cloaks are of the opinion that very little can be done to improve the unsurpassed excellence that the place enjoys already. In many a revealing conversation you will detect an unresolved conflict between envy and self-esteem. As an old lady in one of the most hideous Naples slums once remarked to me, rather snootily, "It's where you were born that counts," and she hobbled away into the fetid, cluttered compartment that was her dining room, kitchen, bedroom, and bathroom, with all the dignity that springs from an ancient heritage and the conviction that comes from the long, full years of a lifetime in one of the great cities of the earth.

Sometimes this dogged devotion to the status quo has to it something far less engaging, something dark and eerie and threatening, like a gas in the air. I once stayed for a few days in the Sicilian town of Partinico, south of Palermo, and felt very strongly this old dark secrecy of the land. In the early morning, when I strolled onto my balcony, the prospect before me seemed altogether delightful. All looked innocent but exotic, fresh with country smells, sunshine, farmland sounds, and rushing streams. The mottled vineyard plain, picketed with cacti, ran away to the distant metallic blue of the sea, and all around, the villages started into clarity as the sun caught them—Montelepre crowned with its Norman fort, Borghetto a medieval tumble astride the Palermo road. The farmers clattered and creaked down the lane beneath, their horses gay with feather tufts, their carts gaudily painted, and when they caught sight of me, perched there in my pajamas above the lane, their steady quizzical gaze of assessment would resolve itself, as likely as not, into a discreet flicker of the hand and the glimmer of a Sicilian smile. Such were my mornings. But in the evening, when I returned to my balcony again, a very different sensation used to overcome me. Then a drear, disquieting mood seemed to fall upon that lovely landscape. The hills seemed to crouch menacingly about the plain, and the villages, so charming in the morning sun, now looked huddled and forlorn—Montelepre whimpering around that keep, Borghetto clinging to the road as if it were a lifeline. And when the sun fell, all was silent, clamped and empty, for old legacies of fear and malaria send the Sicilian peasant home with the dusk and leave the countryside deserted.

The south is full of such chill suggestions, the niggle in the mind or the shudder down the back. This is a territory of dark complexity, very old, very deep, very hard to understand. The farther south you go, the more webbed and private the ambience feels. The Italian south seldom makes itself clear. Its doors are often locked, its shutters often down, and it feels as though, for all the accretia of history littered about the landscape, it has preserved some pungent indigenous essential, some local *casticismo*, undiluted down the centuries. In the big cities especially you may feel this sense of glazed detachment. To the stranger, the urban citizens are usually charm itself, whether they are swaggering past you in snap-brim hats or sitting demurely at their sewing on kitchen chairs beside the road. In slithery Sicilian or jazzy Brooklynese they direct you kindly to your destination, deploring the economic situation or reminiscing about life in Soho, and they are quite likely to offer you a cup of coffee or advise you how best to circumvent the traffic regulations. They are very assured, especially the men, very generous with presents and suggestions, often florid and sometimes condescending; but for all their affability, they often seem to preserve a strange inner reticence, as though their minds are half on the way to the railway station but half upon some immemorial preoccu-

The Road to Huddersfield:

pation of their own, a pagan anniversary, perhaps, or some wild ritual of blood brethren.

This leaves a strange taste upon the visitor's palate, as though his gumdrop has been soaked in vinegar, and it makes him feel as though he is in the presence of something much older and more unyielding than history. The southern Italians move with an almost contemptuous familiarity among the silent monuments of their past—the heavenly white amphitheaters high above the sea, the slender Greek columns alone among the sage, fennel, and mountain orchids. Sometimes you may see a face in Bari or Salerno, across a coffee bar or underneath an exhaust pipe, descended direct from Praxiteles; often a black Arab eye returns your scrutiny, or a Spanish rhythm excites your susceptibilities; but against history the populace seems queerly insulated, like college porters sitting in their lodges, ageless and imperturbable amid the ever-shifting student flood. One evening at Segesta, the most evocative of the Sicilian Greek temples, I heard a young man playing his pipe to a flock of sheep upon the hillside, his wailing chant falling deliciously, like a dying arabesque, upon the scented evening. As I passed his animals, I thought I recognized a familiar tune entwined among those plaintive half-tones, and, sure enough, when I had disentangled the romance of it all from the melodic line, I realized he was playing the old favorite of juke-box and Venetian serenade known to Tin Pan Alley as *Ciao, Ciao, Bambina!*

The Church is one source of the south's stubborn reluctance to look progress in the face. In these remote and simple regions it is not always so clear-eyed and enlightened as it is in Rome; indeed, a Catholic priest once remarked to me in Naples that only three things were necessary to achieve the regeneration of the south: the extinction of organized crime, the establishment of a new ruling class, and the abolition of the seminaries. The Vatican has, I am assured, long since abandoned its early hostility to the Cassa and all it represents; but in the field the beauty of the south's Christianity is still soured by obscurantism. Weird and sometimes terrible are the holy curiosities of Naples, religiously no less than historically the prime metropolis of these regions: the ossuary of Sant' Agostino, where the bones of the departed are prettied up with paper flowers, arranged like shop displays in glass cases and illuminated by electric bulbs (to complete a votive circuit, you buy a plug from the priest on duty upstairs and push it into its socket); or the miraculous congealed blood of San Gennaro in the Cathedral, which turns to liquid three times a year to the sighs and loud prayers of the assembled multitudes, and the ritual curses, vituperations, and insults of the old women entitled to be called "relatives of the saint."

I remember with a peculiar puzzled fascination a festival Mass I once attended in one of the remoter hamlets of the south, a place discarded, like a pile of old rubble, high in the stony goat-chewed mountains. The church was packed. There were five priests in attendance, and two policemen by the door, and a myriad thin, restless children, and beggars in tattered black cloaks, and withered worthies clearing the phlegm from their throats, and hundreds of arthritic rapt-faced women, and girls in kerchiefs looking virginal but sadly undernourished. The church stank of indigence and old clothes; beside the altar, the golden-robed priests moved purposefully

The Road to Huddersfield:

to and fro in the swift counter-marchings of their rite; and so strangely trancelike did the atmosphere feel to me that day, so timelessly suspended upon an alien plane—so muffled did the building seem, for all its rustling and coughing and fidgeting children, that I felt altogether out of my depth. The Church is many things in the south. It is the voice of a sublime belief. It is the abetter of primitive fancy. It is the political party in power. It is the greatest of landlords, for because of the Concordat between Mussolini and the Pope, its estates are not subject to land reform. It is the unappeasable opponent of birth control, which could do so much to ease the anxieties of the south. It is comfort and escapism and discipline, too. It is more liberal by far than it used to be, but it still left me that morning, as I stumbled through the old certainties of the ritual, neither loyal nor iconoclastic, but simply limp.

Violence, too, is a strand in the fabric of the south, laced as always with destitution. This is the land of the Mafia, than which there was never an entity more blurred and camouflaged, more entangled in double-talk. No thorough academic analysis, I am told, has ever been made of this famous phenomenon, for generations the most powerful agency in Sicilian affairs and influential too all over the south—not to speak of Soho or Chicago. Its origins apparently lie in the long subjugation of Sicily to foreign rulers, which forced the islanders to establish their own clandestine authority; but it expanded and changed its character so ruthlessly that toward the end of the nineteenth century, by command of cattle and land markets, by extortion and bloodshed, by an intricate network of secret affiliations, it achieved a stranglehold upon society. The Mafia declined under Mussolini but revived after the war. Today it is more shadowy than ever; but this is perhaps because it is now controlled not so much by raffish scoundrels as by landowners, prosperous businessmen and apparently respectable officials. The Mafia, with all its allied phenomena of bullying and blackmail, stands for everything secretive and reactionary in the life of the south, and its tenets are fundamentally opposed to all that is necessary to the technical revolution—except perhaps a taste for profit. Mafia and Cassa do not mix; for the Mafiosi lurk like ne'er-do-wells along the Huddersfield road.

Ignorance comes next in this roster of obstacles: ignorance inescapable, because there are not enough schools; ignorance of the fatalist kind, which does not try to know. The horizons of the south are far wider than ever before, but there is still to the simplest people of this land a dulled acceptance of the thesis that some folk are created happier than others. Perhaps it is partly the malaise of malnutrition and the lingering effect of malaria. Perhaps it arises from the Muslim hegemonies of the past (certainly there is something sandy and desert-like to the old hill villages of the south, perched like flocks of emaciated birds on arid ridges or pinnacles). Often enough, indeed, the towns of the south greet you nowadays with movie houses and neon lights; but many more remain so barren and vacuous, emanating such an acrid sense of listless boredom, that when I drive into their lifeless squares, searching vainly for a bed, a meal, or a lively face, I am reminded dreadfully of Zagazig, Benha, and the nightmare junctions of the Egyptian Delta.

The Road to Huddersfield:

Bustling reformers can only be affronted by this sense of froward withdrawal. Southerners have a habit still of refusing to recognize that we know better. They still tend to think that land is some kind of mystic commodity, something beyond the ordinary processes of commerce, and not to be irreverently bandied about like spaghetti. They still like to divide it up among their heirs, a portion to each, so that holdings are whittled away down the generations into scattered and impracticable fragments. (At the village of Cutro, in Calabria, the 10,000 acres of agricultural land is divided into 9,000 widely separated holdings, and there are many properties in Sardinia that are only large enough to bear three olive trees.) Southerners often prefer, against all the evidence, medieval methods of agriculture to the latest mechanized techniques, and they sometimes stubbornly refuse to vary a diet unimpeachably proved to be deficient in several essentials. (Most poor southern peasants live on bread, oil, and beans, with *pasta* perhaps once a week, and in the cities of the south, many children eat literally nothing but *pizza*.) Babies are often breast-fed until they are two years old, because their mothers know no other means. Manure is often burned as waste, because the peasants have never learned its use as fertilizer. It is an awesome fact that the Sardinians, in all the slow centuries of their history, never once thought of pruning their own olives—a practice which, since it was introduced to them a few years ago, has quadrupled their production (though it is not in fact true, as one of my more imaginative informants suggested to me, that only within the past decade have they accepted the edibility of the carrot).

All these impalpable hurdles have delayed the progress of the Italian south, and have made this a quicksand situation—more illusory and will-o'-the-wisp, I suspect, than the World Bank likes to suppose. H Street loves to think in terms of before and after, but the dividing line in the Mezzogiorno is hazy and wobbly indeed, and the most eminent Italian specialists often disagree about its position.

There is no denying, of course, that a great deal has been achieved by the Cassa—far more than has ever been achieved before by any of the innumerable transient schemes for the proper unification of Italy. It has been amply proved, in the first place, that the social and psychological ills of the south are curable. It is only a matter of time, and cash, and opportunity. As Gissing said, examining the miseries of the world around him: "Put money in thy purse, for to lack the current coin of the realm is to lack the privileges of humanity." When I dropped that woman in Calabria (she lived in a red railway house beside a level crossing), she asked me for some small memento of our acquaintance. "Can't you offer me some small gift, signor, some small souvenir from England?" "Only the memory of our meeting," I said churlishly, opening the door for her—and she shamed me then by pressing into my hand a large and rather unappetizing bar of nougat.

For this is a decent and diligent people, for all its first impressions. There is nothing wrong with it that coin of the realm cannot cure, if it is properly used, and indeed a whole new generation is already arising that is no longer subject to the harsh old laws of the south. It is only in moments of tired testiness that the foolish foreigner now scoffs. It has been repeatedly proved, especially in the past ten years, that

The Road to Huddersfield:

there is nothing congenitally inferior about the southerner. He need not be abandoned, as the traditionalists like to think, twirling their mustaches, to the "natural poverty of his kind." Southern intellectuals have always been pre-eminent in Italian life; Pirandello, Croce, d'Annunzio, and Lampedusa were all born in the Mezzogiorno. Southerners have long dominated the universities, the civil service, the army and navy—all those occupations where fame or authority is more important than wealth or safety. Today, though, it is being demonstrated that the ordinary working southerner, too, is at least the equal of his northern peer. Workers from Puglia or Lucania put bolts into Fiats as hard and accurately as anyone, and all over southern Italy people really are learning at last, field by field, year by year, the ideas that will take them in the end to Huddersfield. The old people may be stunted still, but the young ones form a different breed—taller, stronger, straighter, livelier than their parents—so that the youngest hunchbacks seem to be middle-aged, and the crippled old crones of the church shadows, the half-wits and the freaks wander through these territories like sad survivors of a dying past.

In material things, too, the south has changed almost beyond recognition—if not in the remotest hinterland areas, at least along the coasts and around the towns. Its poverty is still appalling, but at least it feels a society on the march, after so many centuries of stagnation. As all the warmth of the Cassa's funds is pumped into its arteries, so it seems to be waking from a long, stiff sleep, rubbing the dust out of its eyes. Everywhere in the south you may see the signs of this regeneration. Everywhere you may drive along splendid new roads, thrown across these landscapes with astonishing speed by the masterly Italian engineers. Everywhere you may see the new pumps and aqueducts that are bringing fresh water to the most scabrous of the south's communities. Everywhere you may see the dams and reservoirs that are interrupting the old cycles of agriculture. All along the fecund sole of Italy, where the fields, orchards, and vineyards succeed each other lushly around the gulf from Taranto, you may see the emancipated peasants at work on their own plots, or curse the waspish little three-wheel trucks which, swooping inanely out of gateways piled high with vegetables, pursue their suicidal course toward co-operative prosperity.

Every big town burgeons with scaffolding and steam hammers, so that a haven described in your guidebook as "sleepy, picturesque, and rich in tradition" may turn out to be a rip-roaring, bulldozing, chromium-plated Babel. Every old estate has the row of bleak little uniform houses—each named for a saint, each with a cart or a cow in its adjacent outhouse—that illustrates the progress of land reform. There are new schools everywhere, new forests, new irrigation works, new power stations. Many eroded lands have been restored. Many flood areas have been drained. The splendid Flumendosa dam in Sardinia, a bulging half-circle of concrete like a vast bicycle tire, has already transformed the miserable plain around Cagliari into a prosperous enclave of small irrigated farms, intensively cultivated and producing at least five times as much food as it did a decade ago. The new Campano aqueduct, striding down to the Tyrrhenian from the Matese mountains, not only vastly augments the water supplies of Naples, but actually dives under the sea to take fresh water to the isle of Ischia. Thousands of day laborers, lucky in the past to get three months' work a year, have been turned into peasant proprietors.

The Road to Huddersfield:

Thousands of farmers have been taught how to farm with machines and fertilizers. There is a nuclear reactor north of Naples, and a huge cement plant on the east coast of Sicily, and a steel works at Taranto, and typewriter and car factories in Campania. There are budding chemical, building, and light-engineering industries.

The per capita income of the south has risen by 70% in a decade. They eat twice as much meat in the south these days, use four times as many telephones, drive six times as many cars. There is a healthy movement of people out of the overpopulated, underproductive countryside into the towns. You have only to compare those Cagliari girls, so gay and dapper, with their frowsy elders up the hill to know how many windows have been opened in the south already, and how much light let in.

I wish I could end there, as the World Bank would no doubt like me to ("Peasants everywhere are subject to poverty, ignorance, and disease," one of its experts commented upon this chapter. "A close observation of these phenomena seems to have upset an over-delicate reporter"). Alas, I would not accurately be recording my impressions if I did not conclude on a note of *déjà vu*. Absolutely the south has been marvelously elevated; relatively the gap between north and south remains the same, if it is not actually widening. This does not make the Cassa's efforts any the less admirable, nor the new prosperity of the southerners any the less welcome to see; but insofar as the *problema del Mezzogiorno* is a psychological matter, a sense of separation, inferiority, or neglect, it does mean that the problem remains unsolved. As the Italian commentator

Luigi Barzini has put it, the gulf between *le due Italie* is "a magic gap, which appears to grow wider and deeper as more is done to fill it."

Perhaps the south will never catch up. Certainly the explosion of industrialization has not yet occurred there, and the first sparks of modernism have not yet fired the expected chain reaction. A factory is still a rarity, especially in the southern part of the Mezzogiorno, for the Italian government, despite its lucrative inducements, has not yet induced much industry southward, and the chief industrial investors in these parts remain the State's own holding companies. The south has not yet burst the barriers of its reputation, and industrialists are still chary of a region so poor, so lacking in trained workers and experienced entrepreneurs, entrammeled by such debilitating traditions, with no raw materials and no rich local market and no stable middle class. There is no real labor problem. There is no lack of finance. But there is still a deep-rooted suspicion, an old northern distrust of the character, the integrity of the Italian south: there are two Italies still, and hard-headed businessmen still emphatically prefer the other one.

More people leave the south each year, but the population grows so fast that the ratio between south and north remains roughly the same (since the unification of Italy there has never been more than 38% of the population in the south and never less than 36%). The south still remains absolutely dependent upon the north, still supporting two fifths of the population upon one fifth of the national product. The Cassa has been a noble palliative, but I think it would be rash to suppose that southern Italy will ever support a rich industrial society such as a succession of Huddersfields have created elsewhere in the world. Trade and industry will play a greater part, no doubt, but Palermo will never be another Milan, and Naples, I dare to prophesy, will scarcely change its character in another fifty years.

So, though H Street would doubtless leave the Mezzogiorno with a glimpse of cement factory or reactor, land settlement or power station, I prefer to offer you a last glimpse of timelessness and secrecy—not without a suspicion, somewhere at the back of my mind, that the most destitute of southerners understands more about life than the most padded northern burgher. Let me take you finally to the northwest shore of Sicily, where the coastline of that lovely but disquieting island runs away south to Marsala. There, beneath the village of Scopello, a settlement of tunny fishers lies monastically secluded at the water's edge; and there we shall scramble down, through the sage and the sea anemones and the heaths and the obscure sea-blown brambles, to the clutter of old buildings beside the sea. The place is almost deserted, except in the tunny season, and an air of mystery and reticence issues from the courtyard and huddled buildings.

There are the fishermen's rough barracks, with their bunks and trestle tables, and the score of last year's catches scrawled upon the wall—thirty tunny one day, fifty another, as the anti-aircraft gunners used to record their kills on the walls of their emplacements. There are the great tunny boats, black and brooding in their sheds. There is the little chapel, the roof ominously cracking, and there are the dozens of iron anchors that bear the weight of the tunny nets, and there are the stable-like wash houses in which, a month or two from now, those brawny fishermen, stripped to the waist in the dawn, will scrub the scales from their forearms and the smell of the fish from their chests—all empty now, all silent, all dead, secreted beneath a flowered hillside like a shrine to the sea gods.

Not a brick has changed, not an anchor, not the cut of a boat's prow, for three or four centuries. They fish as they always did, sleep in the same bunks, wash at the same cold taps, pray the same prayers. Who can doubt that they think the same thoughts, too, and cherish more or less the same ambitions? Down at the Scopello tunny fishery you may sense what a wrench the change can be from the private old ways to the public new.

҂ 6 ҂

*On geography, the other Athens,
malaise, geographical grimace,
the Magdalena, period piece,
meaning of a railroad,
Tequendama*

IT IS MOSTLY history that retards the Mezzogiorno, but often enough geography is the obstacle, and sweeping that abstraction out of the way can be a *sine qua non* of Huddersfield. It is only in our own time that the immense continental Powers—Russia, America, China, or Brazil—have been welded into proper nation States, and we have seen how hard it is for a country like Ethiopia to attain modernity when its disparate parts are linked only by rutted mule paths and cart tracks. One of the World Bank's chief preoccupations has been the improvement of communications all over the world, from Australia to Iceland, Japan to South Africa. To see how crucial this particular task can be to the transformation of a State, how closely events often depend upon topography, we will now leap westward to Colombia, the sprawling but still little-known republic that lies in the northwest corner of South America, between the Pacific and the Caribbean, next door to Panama.

The first impression you will get, when your jet screams into Bogota, is one of urbanity, almost of suavity. Here at the

The Road to Huddersfield:

center of things Colombia does not feel at all a backward country. In fact she feels far more sophisticated than any Huddersfield, and several worlds away from Addis Ababa or even Cagliari. Bogota is a finely civilized old city, a little tart, a little eccentric even, with the Andes spilling into her suburbs and her tableland sprinkled with eucalyptus (a tree which, since it first left Australia in 1854, has altered the look of the earth). She feels an instantly individual capital, rarefied and self-sufficient, like an experienced but slightly cranky up-country sage.

Her atmosphere is scarcely exhilarating, if only because she stands 8,500 feet above the sea, making the stranger breathless and the indigene often moody. She is shrouded frequently in the clouds of the high plateau, drenched often in rain, cursed with a climate that has no seasons, but seems to remain perpetually hovering about a damp October. "Look at that lovely summer coming up!" the Bogotan is likely to exclaim, pointing to a patch of watery sunshine on the distant horizon. Her air smells faintly of oil, tobacco, and eau de cologne, her skies are heavy, her colors are browns, blacks, and grays. She is, however, a city of cultivated character: she is infused with Indian blood, and possesses a quality of oriental urbanity that elevates her from the provincial and the prosaic, and makes her a capital of pungent fascination.

Her admirers like to call her the Athens of South America, and she really is a city where any old-school humanist can feel at home. She is rich in good bookshops and comfortable clubs. She is a nest of poets: a lovely place to live, so one Bogota lady told me with a sigh, because every other young man writes you a sonnet. You will not meet many wild abstractionists or atonal composers in Bogota, but you may well encounter sages with an eighteenth-century sweep of interest, dilettantes of prodigious erudition, philosophers of universal range and appetite. I was once introduced to a man in Bogota who had not only translated H. L. Mencken into Spanish, but had also built his own house, written books on cats, English poetry, and celestial navigation, and compiled what is probably the most complete collection on earth of representations of the Annunciation. I asked him where he did his alchemy, as he showed me around his cluttered library, but he answered me only with a frosty kind of chuckle.

All the sting and meaning of Bogota comes from such men of culture, for this is not an exotic city. It is said that its Spanish founders intended to stay there only until the rain stopped. The city's street life is hardly vivid, and for all the Indian women in trilbies, all the resplendent helmeted sentries outside the presidential palace, all the donkeys and tethered speckled pigs in the market place, nobody could call Bogota picturesque. No gay cloaked aristocrats stalk these boulevards, no gaudy tribespeople clatter in from the mountains. Even sin is offered discreetly: "We have pleasure in inviting you," says an impeccably printed card slipped to favored strangers in the street, "to become acquainted with an elegant and comfortable bar, attended by beautiful señoritas, where you will enjoy a fine atmosphere"—and it is signed delicately "The Administration." To the stranger, Bogota seems a gentle and proper place. Her lines are usually orderly. Her pavement crowds are considerate. Sometimes you even see a car, in a moment of rash gentility, give way to a pedestrian.

The Road to Huddersfield:

What is more, this is a capital with an honorable democratic record, not one of your sneaky, sidelong, dictatorial uncertainties. She has had her ups and downs of liberty, Heaven knows, but she is not by nature a repressive, totalitarian metropolis. Her press is free and technically admirable. Her conversations are frank and often libelous. Her secular tastes lean less to the authoritarian than to the anarchical. Her elections are fair, and her ministers, by and large, are not accused of graft. In many ways the Republic of Colombia is both fortunate and advanced. She grows a variety of crops unsurpassed in either hemisphere. She has a highly educated elite, the nucleus of a middle class, rich deposits of gold, platinum, coal, and oil. She commands immense reserves of hydroelectric power, from the numberless streams spilling out of the Andes toward the sea. She is the second producer of coffee in the world. She has lots of room, lots of food, marvelous horizons of unexploited country. She suffers from no smoldering racial antipathies (398 Indian tribes are represented in Colombia, but all but about a million tribespeople have enthusiastically interbred with Europeans). The texture of her everyday affairs is reasonably close-knit, and many of her institutions, from her splendid national airline to her 160 radio stations, seem to work well.

A very different proposition, you may think as you wander through Bogota, admiring the enchanting Catalan observatory, chatting to the intelligent students of the university, drinking superb coffee in a spruce and friendly coffee shop—a different world from Addis, Naples, or even Bangkok. Bogota feels like the capital of a State that long ago built its Huddersfields and has since matured into a genial and

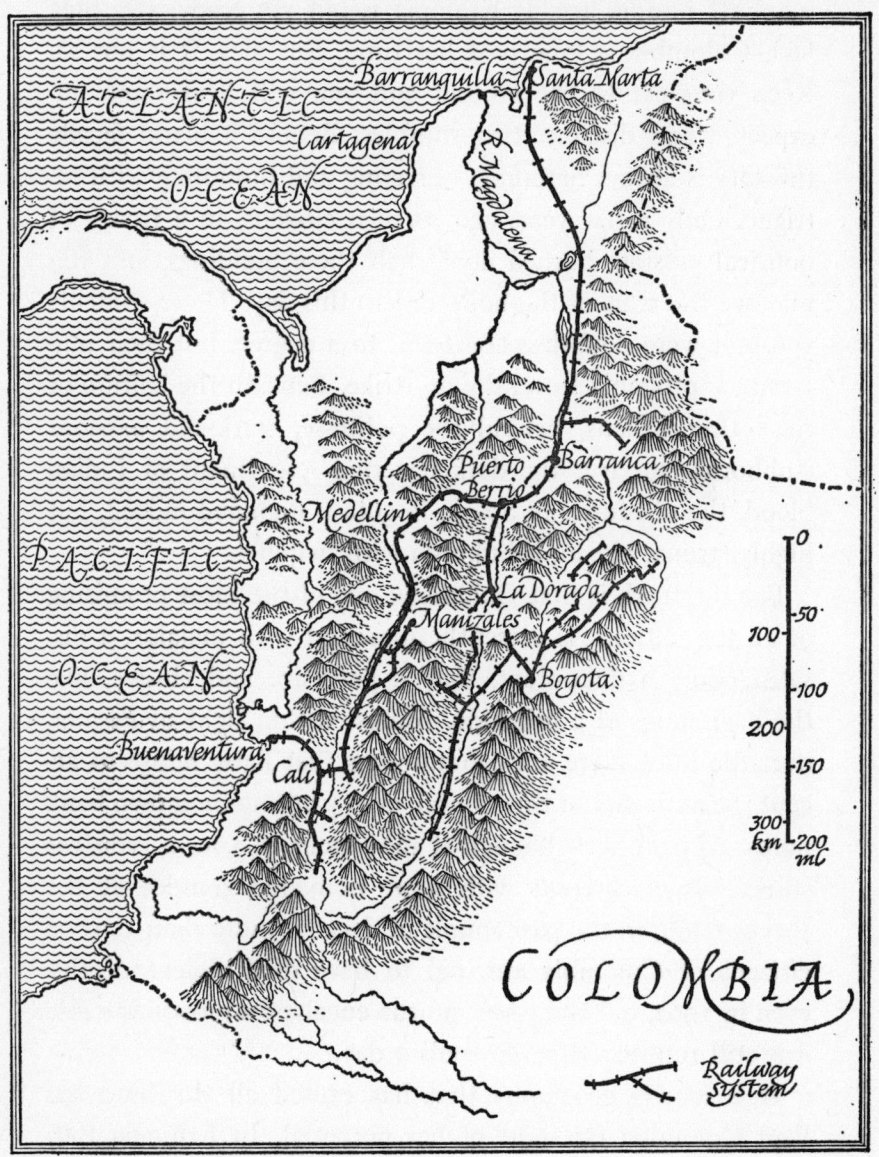

The Road to Huddersfield:

scholarly middle age. If Ethiopia is not yet ready, you may feel, Colombia is long past her time. But alas, it is not so. Keep your ear to the ground and you will hear some unexpected and disconcerting rumbles. Behind a bland façade this city is always brooding, quivering and humming with intrigue. Only a few years ago its own citizens, in a frenzy of political passion, burned down half these buildings, and you may see the scars of the holocaust to this day. Those students you met were doubtless courteous to a degree, but their university is probably frowardly on strike. Beneath the culture of this other Athens, behind the politesse, stark old passions stubbornly survive: the dark festering resentment of Indian blood, the old furies of Spain. Bogota is dignified indeed, but highly strung, like an Edinburgh with twitches.

For the truth is that Colombia, one of the most promising of all the nations, is presently oppressed with malaise—a dissatisfaction, a discontent, that is pervasive and elusive, like the beginnings of a migraine. Almost within sight of Bogota, over the hills, there are communities that flatly refuse to accept the authority of this capital, even printing their own bank notes. And unlikely though it may seem to you, as you eat steak and yucca roots with some pomaded grandee at the Jockey Club, in the past couple of decades more than 100,000 citizens of Colombia are said to have died violent deaths; even in 1962, out there beyond the eucalyptus groves, the rate was still running at seven souls a day.

It is largely geography that has caused all this, and has kept Colombia far short of her potential. In Ethiopia they need the skills, in Siam the popular will, in southern Italy the confidence, but in Colombia, national unity is the first passport to the mills.

"A geographical expression," Metternich called Italy, but the Republic of Colombia is so criss-cross and cut about, so wildly varied in landscape and climate, that I can think of it only as a geographical grimace. Any relief map will show you what I mean. You will observe first that Colombia is divided into two very different halves: to the east the almost deserted flatlands, inhabited chiefly by Indians so untamed that to this electronic day they sometimes dispose of non-residents with spells and poisoned arrows; to the west, where the mountain country forms a bumpy triangle between the Pacific and the Atlantic oceans, the thickly populated Andean provinces, where almost all the citizenry lives. Look more closely, or enlarge the scale, and you will see that this populous region is itself triply split, for here the Andes divide into three terrible ribs, and the country is corrugated by alternate mountain ridges and tropical valleys. So difficult is this terrain that Colombia has always been a collection of several disparate societies, divided one from the other by the enormities of landscape, and often self-sufficient in foodstuffs. The Colombians have always lived in clusters, honoring their own mores and often pursuing their own ends. Some such clusters inhabit the high plateau around Bogota, on the edge of the wasteland. Some inhabit the deep longitudinal valleys. Some live listlessly on the Pacific shore, sweaty and rotted, like backwater communities in a Conrad novel, and some spread themselves happily along the Caribbean beaches, lazy but content at ninety-three degrees Fahrenheit.

The Road to Huddersfield:

Each such cluster is recognizably individual, with its own loyalties, attitudes, and tricks of speech. The Colombians grow wheat, apples, and barley in the middle zones, rice, sugar, bananas, and tobacco in the sweltering lowlands. They range themselves from Indo-Spanish mestizos in Bogota to pure-blooded Catalans in Medellin to gigantic Negroes and mulattoes on the Pacific, and wandering among them is like flicking through the pages of an illustrated atlas. In Bogota the picture often feels obscurely Japanese—somber, rainy, intellectual, and high-cheeked. In Medellin, away to the east, the hard-headed Antioquians have built themselves a little Cincinnati, a city of factories and sober profit. Buenaventura, down on the Pacific shore, is like some gin-soaked West African hellhole, steamy, sodden, and perpetually adrizzle. Puerto Berrio, on the Magdalena River, is like a roistering Mississippi port in its salad days, a place of mules, bandits, dugout canoes, equatorial heat, whores, blaring music, and snorting brass-knobbed wood-burners.

Up on the northern coast is Barranquilla, where the great stern-wheelers reach the sea with their cargoes of oil, hides, and coffee beans. Cartagena, that old glory of the Indies, is a Spanish miracle of ramparts, churches, and piratical echoes. Cali, in the delectable Cauca Valley, reminds me a little of California. And all this is one country—from the celestial snows of the High Sierra to the schooner sails of the Caribbean, from the chill tableland of the capital helter-skelter, within a few miles, down into the deep, damp valley of the Magdalena, all parrots and banana groves. It is rather as though Lagos, Manchester, Havana, and Honolulu were all within common frontiers, speaking the same language but subject to the central authority of Kyoto.

One country, but scarcely one nation. The history of Colombia has been riddled with feuds and separatist jealousies from the moment of her independence to the present day. The different clusters of habitation have often thought of themselves as autonomous entities, free to behave as they please, to follow their own customs, obey their own precepts, and fight their own wars. The settlements were united in liberty by the genius of Bolivar, but they have repeatedly erupted into violent separatism, and the deepest issue in the whole delicate structure of Colombian politics is the dispute between regionalism and centralization, federalism and State intervention.

The two great parties of the State, liberal and conservative, sprang from this fundamental dispute, and to this day feeling between them runs high and sometimes vicious. The precise nature of their differences has long been blurred, so that to most impartial investigators, their principles now seem almost indistinguishable; but in Colombia, as in Gilbert and Sullivan, you are born into one or the other. Their factional fervors extend much wider than politics, and cut the republic asunder. Regions, districts, towns, and families are all passionately partisan, and time and again Colombia has been plunged into civil war. In the nineteenth century there were wars, to name only the more important, in 1854, 1860, 1867, 1885, and 1889. In the conflict that ended in 1902 more than 100,000 men were killed; and one of the most ferocious of them all only petered out in 1953, leaving behind it a habit of violent living and uncertainty. The wars are theoretically over now. A dictator has come and gone since 1953, a military junta has assumed and relinquished power, and today the democratic forms are restored; but it is the rumble of fissiparous dissent that you can hear beneath the surface of Bogotá, the centrifugal instinct, the echoes of old antipathies.

All this agony has stunted Colombia. For all her resources and abilities, she is still a backward State. She is plagued, for all those first appearances, with poverty, disease and illiteracy. On the outskirts of nearly every city you may see the hang-dog slums of the squatters, stumbling in from the countryside in search of Eldorado (the original of which vision, the fabulous "gilded man" of the New World, was supposed to live outside Bogotá). At least half the Colombian children never go to school, and millions of citizens suffer from malnutrition. I once sat for half an hour over coffee at a pavement café in Buenaventura, and never did I see a more piteous citizenry pass by, in the sticky blaze of that tropical afternoon. The waitress, a big, blowsy Negro, wore a flouncy white dress hung loose over one shoulder; the juke box played Sousa marches and flamencos; but the scene in the street outside was anything but jolly. A mutilated beggar crawled about my feet, silently holding out his hand. A shoe-shine boy with a withered arm sat listlessly at the pavement's edge. A few tattered Negroes lounged and slouched about the surrounding tables. Two small boys played football with an old tin can in the street. Sometimes a greasy figure in white ducks shambled into the café, reaching into his money belt for the price of a brandy, and sometimes the beggar scuttled off like a huge black crab to waylay some new arrival, and sometimes the waitress, with a clang of her bangles, screamed some raucous incantation into the kitchen. All around was filth, heat, and degradation, malformations and truncations, stumps of arms and crooked legs and scabbed dry lips.

It is worst of all down there on the west coast: elsewhere the poverty and ignorance of Colombia assume less horrific forms; but it is all part of the national ailment, and one basic reason for it is geography. It is politics too, of course, and selfishness, and the backwash of the past, and economics. But Colombia is retarded mainly because she lacks public spirit, and this is not because the Colombians are a bad people, or a blind one, but because until now the republic has not felt like a unity. How could you feel a national pride when you were daggers drawn with your neighbors over the hill? How could you feel close to Bogota when it required a full-scale tropical expedition to get there? How could you share the aspirations of the next province when it was next to impossible to visit the place, and your whole way of life was different anyway? The very existence of the republic has been described as "an astounding victory of man over nature, and of man over man": it is little wonder that the Colombians, though very far from primitive, are still only halfway to Huddersfield.

The first essential for the technical revolution in this country is an assembly of energies and loyalties, a knitting together, a dismissal of terrain. The World Bank has contributed to many projects in Colombia, one of its liveliest Latin American clients: to agricultural schemes and electric power works, to economic analyses and the development of the delectable Cauca Valley, a lush little Elysium in the western hills. Most of its money, though, has gone to improve transport and communications, and in particular it has gone, like

The Road to Huddersfield:

many an emerald and ingot before it, down the Magdalena River.

There can be few more splendid landscapes on earth than the vast half-explored terrain of central Colombia, tumbling and bumping in gulfs and serrations through thick jungle toward the sea. The first Europeans to see it were the Spanish conquistadors, who built upon the Atlantic shore of Colombia the greatest of their American strongholds, Cartagena. It was a strongbox, a war chest, and a fortress, instinct with all the gun-smoke romance of piracy and conquest, its ramparts seventy feet thick, its dungeons properly barred and fetid, its churches lofty, its gardens seductive, its fortifications so elaborate that King Philip is said to have looked out of his window at the Escorial to catch a glimpse of them, assuming that since they cost so much they must be visible from Madrid.

This tremendous place was only a gateway, built to receive the flow of treasures extracted from the Colombian interior and ship them home in galleons to Spain. Cartagena was only the portal to one of the noblest of all waterways, and one of the least-known to the world at large: the Magdalena River. This great stream was the Spaniards' route to the interior. It was the highway by which the Colombian hinterland was reached, colonized, and developed. It was, within living memory, the only practicable route from Bogota to the sea, the journey taking sixteen days. It has always been crucial to the survival and prosperity of this State, and it remains today a key to the unity of Colombia.

It is less like the Amazon than like the Mississippi. It does not flow through rain forests, tall and impenetrable, but through a scrubbier kind of jungle, thick and hot but seldom majestic. It is an alluvial stream, and it rolls and curls through that exotic landscape in gestures of immense grandeur, now littered with sandbanks, mud flats, and dun islands, now flowing for a mile or two straight, wide, and open, like some organic turnpike. This waterway is the principal unifying factor of Colombian geography. In one sense it effectively divides, with its deep, hot valley, the eastern population clusters from the western; but in another, it does give them all a certain shaky homogeneity. It has always been Colombia's link with the outside world; and if Cali and Bogota, say, were barely in communication with each other, at least they were both in touch with the old river. The immemorial tracks that struggle through the Cordillera nearly all lead down to the Magdalena valley. The sporadic old railway lines of the country mostly lurched and straggled toward its waters, where the steamboats awaited them. Nearly all the celebrated Colombian coffee is carried from the plantations in the temperate zone down the Magdalena to the sea. The Magdalena is not one of the world's longest rivers, but no Nile means more to Egypt, no Ganges to India, than this old stream means to the Republic of Colombia.

The Magdalena traffic is a splendid thing to see, for down these waters there still chug and snuffle in splendor some last survivors of the Mississippi stern-wheelers, long ago superannuated from that most lovable of rivers but here (as on the distant Congo) still as lordly as ever. I once sat on the river bank at Barranca, halfway to the sea, to watch one of these old great-hearts sail by, and a marvelously elevating experience it was. The river is very wide there, and brownish,

The Road to Huddersfield:

and lined with low wooded banks. It was exceedingly hot, so hot that everything around me seemed to shimmer with heat and tropical life. There was a constant humming of insects, and a rubbing of shards, and small weeviling noises in the trees around me, and rustlings and buzzings in the foliage. In the hotel behind me, a place of wicker chairs, beer rings, and gekkos above the bar, I could hear two opinionated locals drunkenly arguing through the afternoon. There were a few small motorboats pottering here and there, with languid men in straw hats propped in their sterns, and sometimes a scruffy small dog barking at the prow. The sky was piled high with magnificent clouds, the water looked lukewarm, all around me was this sense of restless equatorial proliferation, a world of small, irritating, chafing things—and into this fretted, scorched scene there sailed, as proud as any royal yacht, a Magdalena steamboat.

Her twin funnels were belching thick black smoke. Her upper works were a glory of intricate castellation, fretwork baubles, and florid stanchions. An awning was slung over her upper deck, shading her cabins and giving her an air of cool hauteur, like some old paladin smoking his hookah down from Aswan. In her wheelhouse I could see the helmsman, silhouetted beside his great wheel as proud as any Natchez pilot. A powerful bow wave sprang from the barges she was pushing, tossing the small boats at their moorings and squelching into the grass around my feet. From her stern, where the huge paddle wheel ponderously revolved, a fine frothing and commotion of water erupted. In gait she was lofty and precise, rather like an ostrich meticulously treading across an open plain; in style she was triumphantly *fin-de-*

siècle; and so she sailed aloofly past me, with a thumping and thudding of her mechanisms in the afternoon, very tall, very patrician, very beautiful to see.

For a century and more these glorious craft have been the mainstay of Colombia. For passenger traffic the aircraft is now supreme—Colombia boasts the second oldest airline in the world—but most of Colombia's foreign exchange comes from coffee, and for the shipment of this vital crop to the sea, the modern Colombians have relied as heavily upon their Magdalena boats as ever the conquistadors did, shipping their jewels and skins out of the Cordillera to Castile. It has, though, always been a laborious process. This river is pesky with inconsistencies. In the dry season, parts of it are often too shallow for any navigation at all, and at the best of times its swampier reaches are subject to sudden shiftings, so that often you will see one of those lovely stern-wheelers ignominiously aground and desperately trying to refloat herself with clankings and billows of smoke.

When the river is low, traffic is piled up miserably at the ports: delivery dates must be abandoned, and commodities ferment, rust, go to waste, or are lost to thievery. Even when things are normal, the route of a sack of coffee from plantation to percolator has until recently been absurdly involved. It probably went by mule from the grower to the wholesaler, in the coffee metropolis of Manizales. From there it traveled by cableway to a town called Mariquita, on the bluffs above the river (where, half a century ago, some British residents laid out the first 9-hole golf course in Colombia). Thence it went by railway to the river port of La Dorada, and finally by sea-going ship to New Orleans or New York. When

The Road to Huddersfield:

the river was dry, the arrangements were more complex still, for the coffee then went by railway westward to the Pacific, to be shipped at enormous expense through the Panama Canal to the Atlantic coast of North America. Indeed, there have been times when freight from one part of Colombia to another has had to go via Panama, just as the Peruvians, wishing to visit the interior of their country, often used to go to Liverpool to take a ship up the Amazon. The Magdalena has always been an invaluable river, but ornery: strong, but temperamental.

The World Bank found itself paddling in these waters in 1950, when the first of all its general survey missions paid a visit to Colombia and produced a report about as long, and almost as intricate, as the Old Testament. This mission suggested, not only that a series of transverse roads should be built, linking the separate clusters across the grain of the country, but also that a railroad should be thrown down the line of the Magdalena River, replacing those arrogant old steamships at last and ensuring reliable traffic all the year round. Such a line would also link all those scattered patches and snatches of railroad that came down to the river independently, like animals to water, connecting the high settlements with the steamboat routes. It would mean that for the first time trains could run between Bogota and Medellin, the two principal cities of the interior. It would thus weld together the communications of the republic, bolster the sense of national entity, help to reconcile the centrifugal energies of the place, and give Colombia a recognizable jerk in the Huddersfield direction.

The plan was not unanimously acclaimed. Many people

thought a road up the river valley would be wiser. Many others thought it was only necessary to bridge the gap between those parts of the river that were always navigable anyway. To this day many sensible men in Colombia consider the project an error of judgment, and maintain the old Magdalena service to be perfectly good enough. The Bank, however, approved the idea, and, after inspecting the whole Colombian railroad system with a critical eye (noting that a fifth of its locomotives were always out of commission and making sundry recommendations for their improvement), they lent a very large sum of money for the building of the line. Today the Atlantic Railroad is open, and trains are running all the way from Bogota to the Caribbean. Whether or not it succeeds in all its objectives, it is to my mind one of the most spectacularly interesting projects of our time, and one of the most exciting things to see in all the Americas.

You must imagine, as you envisage this work, a situation something akin to the most violent days of the Old West, when the Union Pacific line was pushed laboriously across America in defiance of Indians and desperados alike. The Magdalena valley was always a rip-roaring place, with its rowdy river ports and steamboat stations, and during the construction of the new railroad it was also in a condition of ferocious lawlessness. Gangs of heavily armed bandits, toughened and bestialized by years of guerrilla war, roamed the area, and when the American railroad engineers started work, they found the valley to be in a state of justifiable jitters. One American wife arrived at Barranca for the first time in the middle of the night and went straight to bed: the very first

The Road to Huddersfield:

thing that met her eyes the next morning, when she woke up in her room at the water's edge, was the mutilated body of a man floating downstream with a machete embedded neatly in his belly. The building of this railroad, entailing 500 miles of engineering through mostly virgin jungle, was a tremendous technical challenge; but to all the hazards of work in a brutal tropical climate were added very real dangers of bloodshed and skulduggery, giving the whole operation a fine period flavor.

This suggestion of old-school adventuring was always in my mind when I traveled down the line of the valley to watch them at work, for it is a countryside that looks designed for illicit derring-do. The southern part is mostly uninhabited: a dense, meshed tangle of dark-green foliage, only occasionally intersected by streams meandering down to the great river or by the desolate clearings and mud huts of Indians—as tough and daunting a territory as you could conceive, where monkeys and parrots abound, and blue macaws, and delectable pink herons, meditative upon the mud flats. Downstream, however, the valley opens out and becomes a sort of wide savanna, tawny in color, with huge patches of swamp where the cows stand up to their shoulders in water, and the sun gleams through the soggy grass as though it is not in the sky at all but buried somewhere beneath the squelch.

Mile upon mile this superb landscape extends, speckled everywhere with squat, round trees, so symmetrical and growing in such neat endless parade that it looks like some gigantic travesty of a park, laid out by armies of megalomaniac gardeners. Sometimes you may see the fencing of a vast ranch, with a watch tower on guard against rustlers and squatters. Sometimes you pass a huddled settlement of thatched mud huts entwined in yuccas, shaded by huge banana groves, with mules tied up to their hitching posts in the square, and stocky men in straw sombreros brandishing three-pronged whips or gloomy at the tables of beer shacks.

Sometimes you may see an oil rig hidden in the woods, and a road running away to the river bank. Sometimes a flock of queer birds flashes across your vision, or there is a weird trumpet cry out of the forest, or a flash of summer lightning. Often you see no living thing at all, mile after mile, hour after hour. But always that great river plunges northward, weaving its passage through the wilderness, out of the stifling jungle into the glorious pampas, until at last you see the first blue glimmer of the Caribbean in the distance, like the sheen of the Venetian lagoon, and high, high above you to the east, a cool benediction through the clouds, the distant white snow peaks of the Venezuelan Sierra. It is a marvelous and terrifying piece of country, only waiting to be exploited, and through it, confident and resplendent as any Roman road, the Atlantic Railroad marches, from La Dorada in the south through six degrees of latitude to Santa Marta in the north, from the tropical claustrophobic swelter of the Colombian interior to the coral shore of the Caribbean.

The railroad age is over, alas, but to this day nothing can beat a new railroad line as an expression of change, of push and bustle and ruthlessness, of all, in fact, that takes a people to Huddersfield. I felt this ambience all too strongly at La Dorada, where the new construction began, when some of the railroad men took me for a beer in the main street of the place. As the nineteenth-century visitor to Chicago was told,

The Road to Huddersfield:

it was clearly "no sissy town." Splendid cowboys swaggered all around us, with authentic bad men's slouches, and unshaven faces looked out from the swinging doors of saloons, and sometimes, way down the empty sun-bleached street, we observed a loutish drunk staggering toward us, sombrero on the back of his head, muttering scurrilities to himself and periodically pausing to hitch up his sagging pants.

At every other window, it seemed to me, a painted prostitute simpered, sluttish and gaudy, and every few minutes a platoon of soldiers tramped by, steel helmets tilted over their eyes, but still managing to convey, in the bottom half of their faces, expressions of unyielding ferocity. Sometimes there was a clatter of plates and harsh laughter from the officers' club around the corner; down at the depot the old steam trains snorted in desultory shuntings; from the end of the street, where the spindly smokestacks of the stern-wheelers stood, came the wheezing and groaning of derricks, and the oily, greasy, sweaty, sack smell of the waterfront. "Yessir," said my companions heartily, "quite a place to build a branch line."

It was railroading in the classic manner, such as Brunel would have relished (for that flamboyant engineer so loved the blast and gusto of his profession that he refused to give his locomotives numbers and instead called them only by the most high-flown titles—*Sultan, Pasha, Emperor, Lord of the Isles,* or *Iron Duke*). All along the line, north from La Dorada, you may see the little wooden crosses that commemorate deaths on the job—some by accident, some by plain murder. The construction camps down the valley were like little fortified settlements, with armed sentries, and barbed wire, and notices tacked to the trees forbidding fraternization with bandits. It was rough, dangerous, and exciting living. The very survey route had to be hacked out with machetes, yard by yard through the wet undergrowth, and for hundreds of miles an earth causeway had to be shored up in the swamp. There were landslides every rainy season. There were delays of politics, of climate, of subsidence, of disease, of violence. Nobody seems to know how many men were killed, but they were certainly numbered in hundreds. It is ironical to realize, remembering the calm H Street origins of this venture, that possibly not since Henry Flagler threw his line down the Florida Keys, in the teeth of a whole succession of hurricanes, has a railroad cost so much in human lives.

But it was done. Today it is a line fit for any *Pasha* or olive-green *Sultan*, puffing up to Paddington. It slices clean and majestic through all that tumbled landscape, faithfully following the line of the river and carrying its trains in twelve hours from Bogota to the sea. It took eight years to build, and there is no more telling testimony to the excitement of the World Bank's motion of revolution. What a world away it seems from the bland black waiters in the H Street restaurant to the whores of La Dorada!

Like all railway lines, it commands enormous implications. Already the first settlers have arrived in that rich wilderness in the north, hacking out their homesteads, wiring their ranches, building their own lonely halts beside the railroad track. Already, for the first time in Colombian history, freight is traveling by rail from east to west across the country. Already new currents of life and prosperity are flowing along

The Road to Huddersfield:

this new artery into the veins that spring out of the valley into the several regions of Colombia.

All over the republic you may feel a warming and a tentative blossoming. In the Bogota plain, scores of factories are rising among the eucalyptus trees, fed by new power stations and cherished by this new tautness and speed of contact. The Medellin valley has become one of the busiest and most advanced industrial regions in the whole of South America, and the valley of the Cauca, a sheltered enclave of fertility, is being developed systematically as a unit, as the Tennessee Valley was developed thirty years ago. Not all this burgeoning activity springs from the Atlantic Railroad, but it does all seem part of one organic process, one emergence or release. Of all the situations we have examined, this seems the nearest to that catalytic moment of change when growth becomes the natural order of things, and everyone shares its benefits. My own feeling in Colombia was that only some more violent jolt or stimulant would dispel the old unease of the country; but certainly if you go to the right place at the right time, in the right frame of mind, with the right companion, looking the right way, you may feel that this republic is, if not actually over the hump, at least beginning the long slog up to it.

If so, and if this country's admirable talents can be properly disciplined and laced with finance, then Colombia could be a pace-maker among the lesser South American States, all groping spasmodically toward their Huddersfields, nearly all clients of the Bank: for here, more than anywhere else on earth, you feel the futility, the unnecessary misery of poverty, and the dead weight that geography can be. South America is a continent of infinite resource, bursting with every kind of mineral, sprouting every sort of crop, the kind of place the old pioneers used to dream of and the prospectors conceived only in their most unconvincing tall stories. Yet it is also the scene of some of the most degrading poverty in the world, so that the terrible *barriadas* of Lima lie on the outskirts of that luxurious city like scabs on a fair skin, and the tin roofs of the *favelas* lend a sad irony to the splendid panoramas of Rio.

Like Colombia in macrocosm, South America is not yet a unity. She too lives in strips and clusters, and vast terrible landscapes separate one from another. There are people all around the periphery of the continent, but in the middle there is mostly emptiness, and nothing in contemporary travel is more overwhelming than the rolling half-inhabited immensity of the place. In South America there is emptiness always over your shoulder, behind your back, upstream, or across the mountains. Most of the unimaginable wealth of the continent exists only in economists' graphs or geologists' assurances, because so far geography has kept them tantalizingly out of reach, in the wild and inaccessible hinterland. In country after country, from Brazil to Peru, you will find that only now, like timid settlers edging away from the waterfront, are the people pressing at last into the interior, and symbolizing their new ventures with noble landmarks like Brasilia or bustling inland markets like Santa Cruz in Bolivia.

For here more than anywhere it is fragmentation that is the snag, with its concomitant lack of public purpose. We have seen that patriotism, which is only a politer word for nationalism, is a prime essential of technical revolution. The North Americans, faced with a tumultuous gallimaufry of

The Road to Huddersfield:

immigrants, deliberately kindled their own fire of patriotism, a furnace of flags, eagles, salutes, and sentimental songs, to bring their great nation finally to the boil. The Russians are having to do the same, as they embrace within a Communist society all the Uzbegs, Mongols, Tatars, and Kazaks of their eastern empire. In South America, nationalism has often ridden high enough (in the 1860's there was a war between Paraguay and her neighbors so ferocious that more than half of the entire Paraguayan population, men, women, and children, were killed). However, it is all too often a hotheaded and ephemeral kind of national pride, not deep or consistent enough to produce those qualities of self-effacing diligence that a growing nation needs of its administrators. It is something much more generous that South America wants—the submergence of factional aims and selfish ambitions, the shrinking of great spaces.

Cynics often suppose that it can never happen, that no numbers of roads, railroads, or fertilizer plants can save a continent hopelessly sunk in half-cock jingoism. It will never work, they say, this ramshackle prodigy of a region. Its bigwigs will never keep their appointments, its politicians will never mature, its workers will never pool their loyalties, its undergraduates will never grow up. There must be, they suggest, some debilitating poison to the soil, the water, the climate of the place, and its posturing pseudo-heroes will never give way to honorable and selfless men of affairs. Its Indians will never emerge from lethargy and despair. Its last coup will never splutter, its last tinsel dictator will never sail away to Lisbon, its last tasseled general will never lay down his baton or bludgeon of office.

But I do not believe it, and I do not accept the thesis that only bloody revolution can force South America out of its dismal historical ruts. I am convinced that step by step, dam by dam, year by year, social and political maturity will advance with the progress of technique. One cannot succeed without the other, just as true public spirit cannot be fostered without a sense of unity. They like to say that Brazil has been the Country of Tomorrow for half a century and more; but take a trip down the Atlantic Railroad in Colombia and you will no longer feel inclined to sneer at this astonishing continent.

For, though Colombia is a confused, even a sick country today, she has some seeds of greatness in her, and in their germination you may perhaps see the future of South America, too. It is only a few years, to be sure, since a Colombian dictator imported from Europe an entire power station simply to provide electricity for his own native village; but such vulgar excess does not at all express the character of Colombia. More than most such States, she is blessed with a sense of balance. I was once taken by an eminent Colombian engineer to see the site of a new hydroelectric station, itself financed partly by the World Bank and designed to relieve Bogota's chronic power shortage. This delightful man took me conscientiously but perhaps rather hastily around the works, showing me a pipeline here, a power house there, and sliding astutely but still accurately over the statistics of the thing. He then drove me farther upstream to show me where the same river, tumbling out of the Bogota plateau, falls in a ferocious cataract to the tropical ravines below. We had to wait for the mist to clear, for that day the place was shrouded

The Road to Huddersfield:

in swirling dankness, sliding through the trees and rolling all about us, but presently a small open patch appeared in the vapor and swung into the valley. We watched it as it approached us, like an eyehole in the fog, down the hillside and across the tangled foliage, until just for a moment or two, as it swept down the ravine, we caught a swift glimpse, as through a shutter, of the Tequendama Falls. Nothing anywhere in the world has given me quite such an impression of savage and exuberant power. It looked less like a fall than an eruption, for the river flowed with such ferocity that when it came to the lip of the plateau it threw itself magnificently into the void, like the rain-water gushing from some gigantic gargoyle spout, so furiously that it did not scatter into flying spray, all rainbows and lacy reflections, but fell in a sullen, solid, angry mass, with a grim roar, violently into the abyss.

In a moment or two that gap in the mist passed, we could see Tequendama no longer, and I waited to hear what the engineer would say. I half expected some self-congratulatory assessment of kilowatt hours, but I underestimated the man, as many a transient visitor underestimates his country. He stood silently for a moment and then, turning back toward our waiting jeep, he said, "I think you will agree that a second of that waterfall is worth an hour of any power station on earth"—and so, gently letting out the clutch, he drove me thoughtfully back to Bogota.

7

*The Punjab, aftermaths of empire,
the Garden of India,
partition, eight years' talk,
the treaty, at Attock*

LIKE a great green bowl among the deserts stands the region called the Punjab—Land of the Five Rivers—where five big tributaries join the Indus in its stately progress toward the sea. This is one of the earth's heartlands. To the north extends the supreme mass of the Himalayas, ridge behind ridge, peak above peak, crowned with perpetual snow and marching in ripple after ripple from one end of the horizon to the other: Hindu Kush into Karakoram, Karakoram into Kailas, Kailas into the distant giants of Nepal, Tibet, and Sikkim. They stand there like a frame around the Indian scene, from Afghanistan at one end to Bhutan at the other, and out of them the Indus tumbles to water half a continent. It flows swiftly at first, as it begins its 1,800-mile journey to the Arabian Sea, but as it ages, so it grows in style and stature, until its motion is slow and stately indeed, and its route majestically meandering, and it sometimes declines in altitude only one foot in each mile. It is the basin of this river, joined by the Jhelum, the Chenab, the Ravi, the Sutlej, and the Beas, that forms the Punjab, one of the crucibles of history.

The Road to Huddersfield:

It was in the Punjab that the legendary Indus civilization flourished, creative and urbane, thirty centuries before the birth of Christ. It was by way of the Punjab that Alexander the Great spilled into India out of Persia, on his way to rule the world. It was through the Punjab that the Mogul conquerors came to erect their noble mosques across India and set up the Peacock Throne, studded with a thousand rubies, in the pavilions of the Red Fort in Delhi—"If there be a Paradise on the face of the earth, it is this, it is this, it is this!" It was as "Lion of the Punjab" that Ranjot Singh presided over the astonishing Sikh Confederacy, with its French and Italian generals and its warlike pomp. It was in the Punjab that the mystique of the British empire was pre-eminently established, where Kipling edited the *Civil and Military Gazette* at Lahore, where Gunga Din flourished, and the topewallahs, where Skinner's Horse stabled their mounts in 'Pindi, and the governor spent his summers among the parasols of Murree. It was over the Punjab that the bloodiest of the religious battles were fought, when the British left India and the continent was divided. And it is in the Punjab that the World Bank has achieved the most unexpected of its coups, and made its most original contribution to the wealth of nations.

This book has been full of the aftermath of empire, if only because it is largely the collapse of the colonial system that has propelled the world into the Huddersfield frame of mind. Since World War II, economic development in the backward countries has been inextricably linked with anti-imperialism: the new patriotisms of Africa and Asia have not only urged their peoples forward into modernism, but have simultaneously, and paradoxically, denied them their old sources of investment capital. The decay and discredit of those immense imperial structures has brought with it many exhilarations but many problems, too, left many a proud entity high, dry, and petulant, hijacked many an infant State prematurely into prominence.

It has all happened so suddenly. I myself can remember, as a small boy, contemplating with what must have been a most displeasing complacency the huge red slabs that marked the British empire on the map: and in the 1960's it is difficult to remember that only a couple of decades ago one of the commonplaces of political morality was the notion that men of one race had not only the right but often actually the duty to govern men of another. Today the idea of the "white man's burden" seems as outmoded as the Ptolemaic view of the universe or the divine right of kings. Yesterday it was among the facts of life.

Of course the empire-builders themselves had mixed motives—motives commercial, evangelical, strategic, or frankly emotional. Sometimes they thought of their colonies primarily as sources of raw materials, sometimes as markets for their own manufactured products. Sometimes they were looking for space—seeking a country, as the Boer trekkers used to say, "where you can't see the smoke of your neighbor's chimney." Sometimes they were looking for wealth: some of the greatest families of England, Holland, and Portugal owe their power to the enterprises of empire. They were institutions of intense magnetic force, the European empires, attracting humanity around them as the twin poles of Moscow

The Road to Huddersfield:

and Washington attract the two halves of the world today. You have only to visit Singapore or Hongkong, those supreme *entrepots* of the Far East, or Aden in Arabia, or Curaçao in the West Indies, to realize how busily the trade of the world revolved, only half a century ago, about the pivots of empire.

Everywhere the withdrawal of these great organisms has left vacuums and anxieties. The Dutch left turmoil in Indonesia, the Belgians chaos in the Congo, the British tragedy in India, the French war in Indochina. When the British were planning their departure from Uganda, a nation of some 7 million people, it was frankly assumed that in the year after independence, the country would lose 45% of all its doctors, 58% of its engineers, half its policemen, and a terrifyingly large proportion of its teachers, vets, agriculturists, and technicians of all kinds. The flow of imperial money, before the war the chief impetus to development in the tropical countries, has no less abruptly dried up. As late as 1931 the capital of British companies in India was at least four times as great as that of Indian companies. It was imperial money that built the railways, the canals, and the docks of half Asia and nearly all Africa, with the purpose of bringing foods and materials home to Europe and pumping manufactured goods into the colonial markets: and it is largely as substitutes for the imperial moneybags that all the various agencies of international aid, from the Save the Children Fund to the World Bank itself, are acting today.

Nowhere did the end of the empire have more fearful repercussions than in the Punjab, for that Indian province was peculiarly a ward of the Raj. It was there that the British built, in the later years of the Victorian era, the greatest of all

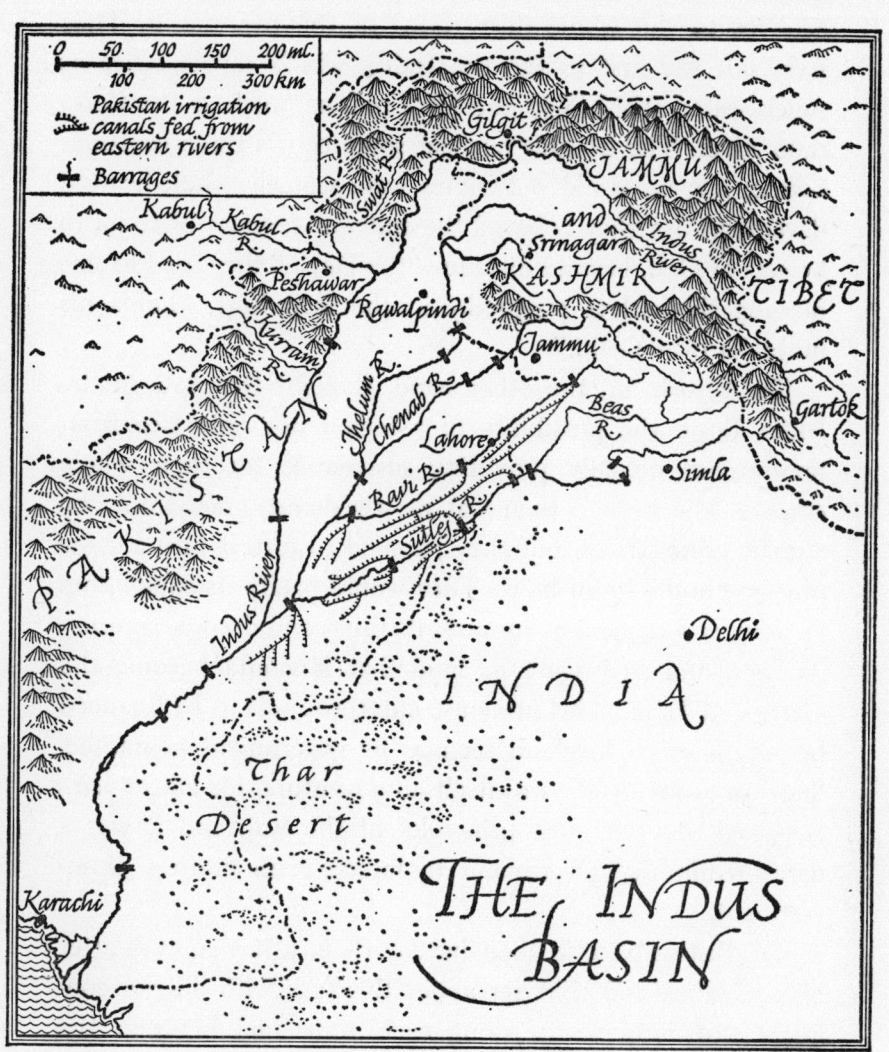

The Road to Huddersfield:

irrigation systems, applying the waters of the Indus and its acolytes to the whole dusty bowl of the river basin. They were not the first to tap the Indus, which carries twice as much water as the Nile and ten times as much as the Colorado River. The Moguls had cut some canals three centuries before; but those old potentates were scarcely whole-hearted developers, for they believed the endemic famines of India to be acts of God, beyond dispute—"the Devil," they used to say, fanning themselves resignedly in the Red Fort, "holds his umbrella over Delhi."

The British, on the other hand, thought they saw in the Indus Basin the possibility of a region not only free from famine but actually providing sustenance for their whole empire. The Punjab then was mostly desert, grazed only by nomad camel tribes, but they planned to turn it into a show province and a grain bowl. They would pacify its squabbling peoples, end its slavery, suppress its thugs and dacoits, simplify its laws, and so irrigate its land that it would become the Garden of India. This immense enterprise was to be financed by capital from England secured by government guarantee. Such an arrangement was itself an adventure, for *laissez faire* governed the economic principles of the Raj, and it was a daring thing for government to intervene in matters of investment.

The British were in their heyday then, just a century after Huddersfield, and they set about this task with all the confidence of supremacy. Along each watershed between the five rivers a main canal was dug, and from it a filigree of lesser channels covered the landscape. The newly watered territories were then divided into separate settlements, and the whole paraphernalia of rural society was meticulously created. Each village was rigidly planned: never more than twelve miles from a market or a railway station, and complete from the start with its own mosques, temples, schools, courts, and police stations. All was built to a plan, like a model village in an exhibition, and started absolutely from scratch. Settlers were carefully chosen and trained, each family receiving a holding of precisely 27½ acres, while the wandering tribesmen of the place were tamed, disarmed, and persuaded into the settled life. The colonists were taught the best way to use land and water, and induced into the proper attitudes of community living. As in the Mezzogiorno of Italy today, so in the Punjab eighty years ago it was not all engineering but sociology, too.

It was a fine pioneering adventure, the bravest attempt made till then to steal a march on mass hunger, and for a time it was one of the great successes of imperialism—conceived on such a massive scale, hustled through with such energy and enthusiasm, that in a matter of decades those irrigated areas had lost the harsh angular quality of newness and had already blurred and blended into the Indian scene. By 1909 this was the most extensive of all irrigation systems, watering an area half the size of Great Britain, or about as big as New England. By 1911 the Encyclopedia Britannica was able to describe the former desert of the Punjab as "one of the great wheat fields of the British Empire." Even the financial risk had paid off: one of the new colonies, the Britannica observed with satisfaction, had already returned nearly 21% on the capital invested. In 1911 the population of the Punjab was 25 million; in half a century it doubled. The

The Road to Huddersfield:

colonies along the Lower Chenab alone, in territory hitherto almost uninhabited, grew so fast that in forty years they supported a population of 1½ million. The Punjab became the most advanced and prosperous of all the Indian provinces, and the patchwork of square green fields, running down from the foothills toward Sind and the sea, became part of the earth's face, organic and irremovable.

It is extraordinary how quickly the ethos of empire has faded, how soon the satraps have lost their accents and the streets their commemorative names, as the whole edifice of a discredited idea crumbles into limbo. When the British look back upon their years of climax they may well think of the Indus, which came relatively late in their imperial career, as the apex of their achievement, the very best of the things they did. More than anything, perhaps, the application of water to the growing of food is a memorial of the great civilizations. When the Babylonian empire disintegrated, so too did the marvelous waterworks of Iraq, and the Land of the Twin Rivers decayed into ignominious squalor. Whenever a weak pharaoh governed Egypt, he let the canals silt up and the irrigation devices rot. If the United States withers at last, I suspect that the tremendous riverworks of the West will longest be admired as physical evidence of her genius. Bismarck, wishing to express his opinion of the feckless Irish, once suggested that they should change places with the Dutch: the Dutch would soon make Ireland a prosperous republic, and the Irish would presently let the Dutch dikes leak and drown themselves. Thus the mesh of canals in the bowl of the Punjab expresses the energies of the British at their strongest and most self-controlled, far more effectively than any tattered battle flag or stately home.

But the triumph did not last, for reasons partly natural, partly political. In the first place, the population overtook the works. When the Moguls built the first Punjabi canals, the population of all India is thought to have been about 100 million. By 1901, when the British canals were nearly complete, it was 294 million. By 1947, when the Raja died, it was about 435 million. The Punjab burst with people, the export of grain declined and finally stopped, and the wheat field of empire was itself, by the 1940's, chronically on the brink of starvation.

At the same time the irrigation system itself showed the deficiencies of its age. For one thing, it was seasonal: it included no storage dams or reservoirs, so that in bad years the canals ran dry, and in good ones half the precious water ran down to the sea unused. For another thing, all those years of irrigation were beginning to waterlog the land. If you look down at the Punjab from an aircraft, you will see here and there below you, splotching the green fields like mold on the wall of an old house, patches of gray decay, rising patternless and ominous across the landscape. This is salination, a rotting of the land caused by a rise in the level of the underground water table, which forces the salts of the earth to the surface and gradually turns fields back to desert. It does not steal inexorably forward, like an encroaching sand dune, but erupts unpredictably in disconnected patches, now desolating a village in Gujerat, now withering away all possible means of livelihood from the farmlands of Shahpur. It reminds me of some nightmare fable of science fiction, so unearthly does

The Road to Huddersfield:

its progress seem to be, and for several decades now it has been nibbling away at the welfare of the Punjab. Today the Punjabis lose at least 150 acres of land every afternoon of the year: even in the last years of the Raj, the British used to say that two or three cricket pitches were going under every day.

Most terribly of all it was politics that desolated the Garden of India and left the memory of empire sour. The conscientious British colonization officers of the Punjab instilled many conventional virtues into their carefully selected peasants—thrift, diligence, respect for the law. They failed, however, to foster the quality of toleration. Men of three religions lived in the Indus Basin—Hindus, Muslims, and Sikhs—and they never did settle their sizzling differences of faith. As in Colombia, on the other side of the world, factional loyalties came first, public interest second, and religious disagreements had hardened into bitter communal antipathies. When the British prepared to leave the sub-continent, after the Second World War, it was the unappeasable discords of the Punjab which, more than anything, decreed the partition of the sub-continent. Differences were so old, so deep, so irreconcilable, and the Muslims were so determined to establish their own Islamic State, that a division somewhere down the religious demarcation line became inescapable.

It was drawn arbitrarily, hastily, some say irresponsibly, for the British only wanted to go home. Its implementation led to factional violence so ferocious that hundreds of thousands of people lost their lives, and the whole of the Indus Basin was plunged in terror. (Nehru himself, touring the Punjab during those awful days, once plunged into a raging mob of

Sikhs and Muslims and beat about him with his fists, so furious was he at the horror of it all, and so despairing at its futility. When the bloodshed died down at last, when the combatants had withdrawn bleeding and sullen, the dust died down, and the incense cleared, it dawned upon the world that clean down the line of that noble grain bowl, dividing one of the great geographical unities of Asia, there stood an implacable armed frontier. Half the Indus Basin lay in India, half in the territories of her defiant enemy, Pakistan; and one of the river barrages upon the border was actually used as a fort.

This is an imperial legacy of the most perilous kind, for nothing is more inflammable than water, nothing more vicious than a squabble over riparian rights. On every level of human conduct, from the neighbors disputing a faucet to the State contesting the flow of a river, the sharing of water is alive with dangers. It is serious enough when the differences are only between neighboring provinces: in the old days Sind and the Punjab had a long-standing quarrel about the use of the Indus waters. It is menacing enough when they are between reasonably friendly neighbors: for years the riparian disagreements between Egypt and the Sudan threatened the stability of northeast Africa, and stymied every attempt to use the full flow of the Nile. But you can hardly conceive a more explosive situation than the one caused by the division of the Punjab, which for some thirteen years threatened to plunge two of the world's most populous nations into war.

The new frontier ran well to the east of the Indus proper, but cut across the flow of the five great tributaries, vital to the

The Road to Huddersfield:

working of the irrigation system. Moreover, since Kashmir too was divided by force of arms, the Indus itself flowed through Indian-held territory before it debouched into Pakistan. The Muslims of Pakistan were left in possession of most of the watered areas; but the Hindus of India were masters of the headwaters, and also of two of the most important feeder canals—themselves as big as fair-sized rivers. India could thus block, if she pleased, the flow of water into the basin, or make whatever use of it she could before a drop crossed the frontier. In theory at least she could dry up the whole intricate canal system of the western Punjab, and leave most of Pakistan helpless. The Pakistanis felt themselves to be absolutely at the mercy of their neighbors, and there is no sensation more conducive to wild behavior.

For a decade and more the two States, each with its own superb army, snarled and bickered across the basin, and the dispute became one of those dour perennials of the newspaper columns, sometimes flaring momentarily into headlines, usually grumbling crossly away in a corner of the page. Both sides were stubborn to a degree: in 1952 indeed the Indians did temporarily block the feeder canals, and for a day or two war seemed a certainty. The issue seemed to be irresolvable, and the Indus appeared to be one of those problems that the world must learn to live with, like the Cold War itself or nuclear annihilation.

By 1951, when the World Bank enters this story, the situation was vicious to a degree, if only because the canal system had by now acquired an importance greater by far than its creators had conceived for it. Of the 50 million people then living in the Indus Basin, 40 million were Pakistanis—and no nation was in a more parlous condition than theirs. Pakistan was governed then by a travesty of a democratic regime, ensnarled in corruption and demagoguery, and she seemed to have no way of earning her own keep. It is a moot point, whether, at the end of British rule in India, ordinary people in that sub-continent lived any better than their forebears did under the Moguls, because all the benefits of imperial rule, all the roads and railways and canals, had done no more than keep up with the ever-expanding population. Certainly by 1951 Pakistan, with a population of almost 80 million, was not far from destitute. She had no steel mills, no reservoirs of oil, no iron ore to mention, no uranium that anybody knew of, no copper, no tin. The Indus valley, which contained almost half the cultivated land of the entire State, could only just support its own people, and in the eastern provinces of Pakistan half the people died before their first birthday. The population was growing by nearly a quarter in every decade, and Pakistan was already among the half-dozen most populous countries in the world.

Nor was she flaccid or resigned beneath these burdens, for all her Muslim faith. The Pakistanis are a marvelously martial people, and the stimulus of new nationhood was always prodding them. They were surrounded on all sides by enemies. To the west were the Afghans, with whom the Pakistanis maintained an old, long-curdled feud. Beyond the Hindu Kush, less than 200 miles away, stood Russia, against whose historical intentions Pakistan was militantly allied. Across the Karakoram, within 300 miles, waited China, that *draco ex machina* of all Asia. And all along the eastern frontier lay India herself, the most immediate and threatening of them

The Road to Huddersfield:

all. Pakistan had been born as an idea—the idea of a State governed throughout by the precepts of Islam—and in the teeth of all these dangers and disadvantages she was still trying to convert that idea into a nationality. She was concerned, not only with water rights and starvation, but also with her survival as an entity, a community, a State. To most of us the partition of India seems a terrible catastrophe, but to the Muslims of Pakistan it still has the quality of an inspiration.

Never did a country seem to need her Huddersfield more—to bolster her confidence, calm her apprehensions, reduce her dependence upon imports, give work to her people, modernize her agriculture. Growth could scarcely be an ambition in such a society, but with all the tools of modern technique, at least survival might be easier. Nothing could be done, though, so long as the Indus problem festered there, and war was a weekly possibility. Nobody would risk money in such a situation, and the Pakistanis themselves, inflamed by patriotic grievances and crippled by vast military expenditures, were hardly in the Huddersfield mood. The Indus system could still be greatly improved, modernized and enlarged, to increase yields and provide the power for industry: but so long as two angry armies glared through their gunsights across it, there was not a hope of progress. As Eugene Black himself put it, "As long as the two countries continue to devote half or more of their annual budgets to military preparedness, this would detract from their ability to borrow and repay loans from the Bank for any purpose at all."

In 1951 it occurred to Mr. David Lilienthal, of the Tennessee Valley Authority, that the Indus problem might best be regarded, not as a political, but as a technical challenge. He envisaged a joint development scheme for the whole basin, straddling that ominous frontier and exploiting the resources of the Punjab for the benefit of Indians and Pakistanis alike. The pooling of energies in so splendid a task, he thought, might induce the neighbors to swallow their acerbities and divert their passions into more constructive channels. These notions he embodied in a magazine article, and there one fine Washington day Black read them, swiveling in his chair before his map, with a particular kind of interest.

In several situations the World Bank has acted as a mediator, for its methods are nothing if not empirical, and it scorns no device to usher a people along the road to the mills —provided, of course, the rules of banking orthodoxy are properly honored. It unsuccessfully mediated between the Persians and the Anglo-Iranian Oil Company, for instance. It settled an old issue between the City of Tokyo and some aggrieved French bondholders. In 1958 it mediated between the Egyptian government and the shareholders of the nationalized Suez Canal Company, and in the following year it arranged a financial settlement between the British and the Egyptian governments—a mission conducted by Black himself "in his personal and informal capacity," which means that he was accompanied only by one vice-president of the Bank and two heads of departments. In 1951, however, the idea of Bank mediation was new, and indeed the very thought of it seemed to confirm the view of that Bretton Woods commission which doubted whether the World Bank ought to be called a bank at all. Black nevertheless adopted Lilienthal's initiative, and invited the antagonists to accept the good offices

The Road to Huddersfield:

of H Street. The consequent negotiations lasted just a little less than nine years, perhaps the longest gestation any international agreement has ever had to endure.

At first the intention was, as Lilienthal had suggested, the joint development of the whole basin. The negotiators who came to Washington were irrigation engineers, and the intention was to reconcile their separate proposals for the use of the Indus water. They met upstairs at H Street under the chairmanship of General Wheeler, one of the most celebrated of American engineers, and curious indeed was the flavor of their discussions. Both Indians and Pakistanis were members of the old Indian Civil Service, under the Raja. They knew each other well, talked the same language, pursued the same interests, only now overlaid by national passions and litigious demands. In the evenings they talked happily about old times; during the day they argued, with an extraordinary intensity and intricacy of detail, about hydrography—and it is astonishing what disparate conclusions can be drawn from the same set of unimpeachable statistics. For a year they tried to agree on the data, and then each side presented a plan for Indus development which was instantly rejected by the other. It was clear that they had reached an impasse, and General Wheeler himself, recognizing that the Indus Valley Authority had become an unattainable ideal, then drew up an entirely different kind of proposal on behalf of the Bank itself.

He suggested that, far from trying just then to restore the unity of the Indus valley, they should consolidate its division logically and then proceed with its development. Each side should have a fair share of its waters, and each should then be encouraged to go ahead with new works. In principle, the idea was that three of the six rivers should be reserved for the use of India and three for the use of Pakistan, and that Pakistan should be compensated by new engineering works for the water she would lose. At the same time, storage works would be built to circumvent the old round of drought and plenty and provide hydroelectric power for new industries. A series of *ad hoc* agreements was patched up to keep things quiet in the meantime, and the negotiators now spent two testy years discussing the details of the proposition and the precise use to be made of the separate waters.

Again the talks bogged down. By 1958, relations between the neighbors were worse than ever. A disastrous summer had intensified the flickering tension of the frontier. Both sides balked at the cost of it all. The Indians wanted some of the new works to be built on their side of the frontier; the Pakistanis insisted they should all be within Pakistan (they already objected strongly to a big dam which the Indians had begun on the Sutlej). The Indians quoted *force majeure*; the Pakistanis quoted the old principle that in riparian disputes the existing uses of water must be sacrosant, and only additional uses are open to argument—by which they meant that if might was on the other side, right was all on theirs. So tricky and ticklish did the negotiations become that the Bank took to dealing with each side separately, one at a time.

But at this moment, toward the end of 1958, history swung around one of its sharper corners. In Pakistan, a military coup swept away the sordid debris of the old regime and brought into power a government that was all brisk, straight, and soldierly. And in Tibet the Indians found themselves

The Road to Huddersfield:

faced by a China so evidently aggressive, so brazenly flexing her muscles, that the idea of a reconciliation with Pakistan suddenly seemed to make much better sense. The talks took a more promising, if scarcely gentler, turn. Discussions were resumed around the table in H Street. Black himself flew out to the sub-continent to meet the leaders of both nations; and in September 1960, after drafting sessions that sometimes lasted from ten one morning to two the next, the Indus Water Treaty was signed. It was, in a knobby sort of way, a landmark in the history of diplomacy, and is certainly the most flamboyant of the feathers in the World Bank's normally somber Homburg.

In the long view of history it may not seem much, for I myself cannot believe that this unhappy frontier will survive many centuries; even the British Raj itself, one of the most vital and forceful phenomena in the whole range of Indian history, lasted from beginning to end, from John Company to the farewell bugle calls, no more than 300 years. In a shorter perspective, though, the Indus treaty and the works it envisages loom grandly, even portentously, over the horizons of contemporary affairs. Not many such agreements have been reached, in the anxious context of our times, and it is said that the engineering works will be the greatest ever undertaken by the brains, brawn, and bulldozers of man.

It is agreed, in brief, that India shall keep for her own use the waters of the three eastern rivers, the Ravi, the Sutlej, and the Beas, and that the Indus itself, the Jhelum, and the Chenab shall be reserved almost entirely for Pakistan. This means that enormous works must be undertaken to transfer waters from the western rivers to those parts of Pakistan hitherto watered by the eastern ones, and at the same time two storage dams are to be built in Pakistan, one somewhere on the Indus, one on the Jhelum. All this will entail a stupendous expenditure of energy. It will be roughly equivalent, as a physical task, to the construction of the Boulder Dam plus the cutting of the Corinth Canal plus the shifting of the entire Egyptian irrigation system from one part of Africa to another. It will mean the digging of eight great canals, some of them more than 200 miles long, one of which will have to pass in a tunnel under a river and several of which will carry ten times as much water as the Thames at Teddington. One storage dam alone will consist of as much earth as you would need to fill in the whole Suez Canal again. The whole scheme will take many years to complete; and the Indians have agreed to allow an adequate amount of water to flow for another decade, provided the Pakistanis try to get the work done by the end of 1970.

As for the cost, it is so astronomical, and so certain to prove an underestimate anyway, that it is scarcely worth recording. If there is one subject on which professional financiers are nearly always misinformed, it seems to be money, and when the treaty was being negotiated, nobody knew within many millions of dollars how much cash would be needed. The available data was meager in the extreme. Details of the biggest single work in the plan, the Mangla Dam on the Jhelum, now fill six sizable typescript volumes, but when the treaty was signed, all that was known about it was contained in one small booklet—and this dam alone will be long enough to

The Road to Huddersfield:

extend from Capitol Hill to the Lincoln Memorial, besides being considerably higher than St. Paul's Cathedral.

The estimates had to be founded on technical supposition no more, and they had to be made in a hurry, for the whole tenuous possibility of agreement, so perilously fragile a substance, depended upon raising the necessary money. In the end it was done spectacularly. The Bank, the impresario or major-domo of the whole affair, agreed to make a sizable loan. India agreed to pitch in. And the United States, Britain, West Germany, Canada, Australia, and New Zealand agreed that between them they would put up a good deal more. This compact was sealed in the Indus Basin Development Fund Agreement, something new and encouraging in the often sordid story of international finance.

Today, at the beginning of 1963, they are putting the treaty magnificently into effect. All over the Indus valley you may meet the engineers, scientists, financiers, and sociologists who have been summoned to the Punjab by so tortuous and protracted a series of events, and by the improbable agency of the World Bank. It might have been an appalling catastrophe, the failure of the Bank's mediation, and indeed by absolute standards it will be a tragedy when it finally succeeds, all this work, all this money, all this emotion, this high intent, this skill, this bustling yellow machinery, this infinite last quibble of legality—all this, only to help split one of nature's grandest unities in two! On a lower level of analysis, though, the treaty is all good. It makes that freakish partition line more permanent, perhaps, but much less harsh. It gives the Pakistanis a healthy lift toward Huddersfield. It helps to prove that riparian neighbors need not always be at one another's throats (though it was long after the agreement, as it happens, that one of the best-known Pakistani newspapers described the Prime Minister of India as "the clay-footed and cloven-hoofed idol of suckers throughout the world").

Not least, it is a triumph of bankers' acumen, what the Bank's speech writers like to call "development diplomacy." The Indus settlement placed the World Bank, already a difficult specimen to categorize, in a new genus altogether. It demonstrated H Street's unforeseen powers as a peacemaker. Fortified now by its reputation for absolute professional impartiality, and by the fact that it had already lent money to both sides in the dispute, it was able to bring to bear upon the conflict instruments quite new to diplomacy. Free alike from the taint of power politics and the feebleness of most international agencies, backed by its unique ability to raise money from the richest and most skeptical sources on earth, enriched above all by its capacity for inspiring a sort of reluctant, backhanded, corner-of-the-mouth trust, the Bank seemed to offer a new dimension in public affairs, something not so false as conventional diplomacy, or so fickle as politics, or so shallow as commerce, but cut to a shape all its own, prismatic on the outside, monolithic within.

The United Nations, like the League before it, is hamstrung because it has no means of enforcing its decisions—no standing army, no tax collectors, no police force, no bailiffs. The World Bank, though, does have a weapon: money. It was the authority of money that achieved the Indus settlement: money commanded by an international agency with no ax to grind, wielded by men of professional financial skill —not diplomatists or politicians, not even heady idealists, but

The Road to Huddersfield:

sensible money men of several nationalities. It was a technician's treaty, in a technical age: the kind of concord a well-disposed computer might arrange if you fed it the right mixture of prejudices.

Somehow it comes very properly out of the Punjab, for this is an allegorical kind of country, and the Indus itself is a river of such character that it is easy to imagine myths and precedents springing dripping from its waters. The best way to approach the Indus is from the west, out of Afghanistan. You skirt the old Lee-Enfield forts of the Khyber, and sidle past the perfumed Peshawar bazaars (where the tongas clip-clop plumed and burnished, and the frontier tribesmen stalk like genies through the alleyways), and presently you reach the scowling watchpost of Attock, where the river bars your way.

Instantly you feel yourself in the presence of a supreme geographical fact. Your highway is invested by memorials to forgotten wars, regimental crests carved in the rock, battle honors and soldiers' graffiti. Across the river a splendid Mogul fort streams down the escarpment to the waters' edge, attended on every hillock, on every watchful ridge, by lesser fortifications, towers, and embattlements. Huge block towers guard the steel bridge spanning the stream, and as you drive nervously past them, a soldier with fixed bayonet inspects you with a cold and speculative gaze. The bridge is closed from sunset to dawn, so a notice sternly reminds you, and when you pass between its heavy girders you can hardly help remembering that Alexander once passed this way, and Tamburlaine, and Nadir Shah, that Akhbar himself built that fort upon the hill, and the imperial British this bridge across the river.

For there is something stirring and high-flown about the Indus, something very big and grand. As you run away up the east bank, hastening off to Rawalpindi and a hot bath, you feel you are leaving behind you some intensely important, incalculably old, ever-pulsing energy, whose dour and fateful passage through history you have, just this once, reluctantly been permitted to cross.

⁊ 8 ⁊

*Still studying ⁊ shortage of clients ⁊
liberal tendencies ⁊ IDA ⁊
plastic Zion? ⁊ back to Huddersfield ⁊
a comfort to end with*

VERY EARLY in many publications about the World Bank you will find a paragraph about the Advisory Council. Under the original articles of agreement this body was established to "advise the Bank on matters of general policy." It consisted of ten experts of such magnitude that one was an ex-President of the United States, two have since become peers of the British realm, and a fourth has been Prime Minister of Peru. It met, however, only twice. Both the Bank and the Council itself agreed that it was a waste of money ("not likely to have a value commensurate with its cost"), and it was thereupon dissolved by a characteristic formula. It was supposed to be elected every two years, and when its first term of office expired, the Bank decided that "the reorganization, selection, duties and all other matters relating to the Advisory Council be studied, and that pending completion of this study, the selection of the new members of the Advisory Council be deferred."

It has been deferred ever since, and the Advisory Council has been consigned to limbo for so long that when Mr. Herbert

The Road to Huddersfield:

Hoover recorded his association with it in *Who's Who*, he even got its name wrong. There is almost nothing, you see, about the World Bank that cannot be changed, dropped, or expanded if the will is there. It is much more flexible than it looks, and its methods and practices have never been reduced to any formal code. We have investigated five situations in which it is at work, all very different in kind as in place: from Ethiopia, where the government once decided to switch the whole road-building forces to the construction of an airport big enough to take Boeing 707's, to Pakistan, where I once read in a manual for Army officers that it was "advisable to take a reasonable interest even in the prisoners locked up in the quarterguard." In each case the Bank's policies, methods, and even intentions have been different, with this one common denominator: the conviction that change is usually for the best, despite first appearances, and that, in the end, all nations must come to Huddersfield.

It began as a Bank, but it shows signs of developing into a philosophy, for the application of solid old Rialto values to the progress of the race has sparked some unsuspected fires. Of course it is still an instrument of capitalism, despite the lively membership of Yugoslavia. The callower American observers still insist upon regarding it as a tool of western diplomacy—"dollar for dollar," *Time* once observed, "the World Bank has proved itself one of the most effective weapons in the cold war"—and the intenser British theorists still call it blinkered and ultra-cautious. Its very success has been based, for all its elasticity of method, upon a rigid set of financial principles, not always generous or imaginative, and governed partly by the fact that it must itself raise money on the ordinary money markets. "We want our money back, and we want it properly used." They are good, straightforward, Yorkshire rules, and it is their enforcement that has induced so much private investment to follow the Bank's writ to so many unlikely destinations.

They do not, however, always fit the times, chiefly because of the standards H Street has set for the aspirant world. As the last of the imperial administrators withdraw, so inevitably there is a slump—perhaps transient, perhaps permanent—in the quality of local governments. The first colonies to gain their independence were those with the best indigenous civil services and the most money; but the African States which are now pressing most eagerly toward the mills are often poor and usually very backward. By its old criteria, the Bank is running out of clients. Many poor countries are "exhausting their creditworthiness"—which means that they are too heavily in debt to get another loan. Others are disqualified for help because they can no longer claim a guarantee from a rich imperial government in Europe. Most African administrators seem to agree that what their countries chiefly need, more than roads or telephones or even power plants, is schools; but it was only in late 1962 that the Bank first modified its refusal to finance education—and then only to make grants for "technical, vocational or other educational projects of a sort closely related to the objectives of the lending activities of the Bank." Nor is it anxious, even now, to support projects that are not potentially profitable ("Mr. A. agreed with Mr. D.," I once read in a Bank memorandum, "that pure water had many valuable side effects, but one could not measure their contribution to production.")

In short, the World Bank has almost priced itself out of its own market, not by the cost of its money, but by the altitude of its standards. It is getting harder and harder to find projects it considers worthy of support, and already the chief difficulty it faces, in a world desperate for investment capital, is a shortage of countries that can afford to get further into debt. It has been suggested that before long the repayments on its old loans, plus interest and service charges, will be equal to the amount of its new ones, so that the Bank will not really be emitting any money at all—a healthy situation indeed for any other kind of bank, but scarcely a proud boast for this one.

Of course the men at H Street are well aware of all this. Most of them are, as their bitterest enemies will admit, anything but fools. The World Bank long ago developed political appreciations of a kind not common in Wall Street or the City, the naïveté of whose normal practitioners can be bleakly measured by the absurd fluctuations of market prices that are sparked by the most ephemeral items of the day's news, the death of a President's uncle, or a silly saber rattle from the Ukraine. The Bank still makes enemies by its distrust of public ownership, but it is keen-sighted enough, and confident enough too, to recognize that in an emergent world that is largely ex-colonial and often curdled by unfair privilege, the old-school right-wing authoritarian, so dear to financiers of a lesser vision, is really a poor risk.

On one level, of course, nobody is a better partner than a compliant dictator. Soothing indeed was the ease with which General Franco was able, on American request, to run a pipeline across Spain, for he was not in the least perturbed by any public opposition nor hampered by commissions of inquiry, courts of compensation, cranks who believed it would be against God's will, or inventors who thought it would be wiser to have a conduit slung from balloons. Marshal Tito has been one of the Bank's more diligent and efficient clients. Successive Siamese despotisms have all worked genially with its representatives. ("As a result of a military coup in 1957," the Bank reported blandly of one of its Siamese protégés, "the chairman of the Board was replaced by the Commander-in-Chief of the Thai Navy.")

More often than not, though, autocracy is bad finance, as a score of discredited despots, from Batista to Nuri es Said, have dismally and sometimes heartrendingly demonstrated. In Colombia the Bank's programs were disastrously interrupted by the emergence of the dictator Rojas Pinilla, whose village power station, when at last the people got rid of him, was used to provide electric light for half a province. For years the Ethiopians' progress toward Huddersfield was impeded by the autarchy of the Emperor, who used to treat the national development as a kind of personal hobby, and sometimes delayed important decisions for months because he refused to let anyone else take responsibility for them. The Bank's loans to South Africa are carefully framed for repayment within ten years, on the supposition that the despotism of *apartheid* cannot last much longer.

The military autocracies of our time, mostly middle class in origin, are often something different in kind: but the old rock-bottom landowning feudalisms are like road blocks on the Huddersfield highway, and are not much loved in H Street. The Bank recognizes that in many countries reform is an absolute prerequisite of progress. Black himself once told the

The Road to Huddersfield:

Economic and Social Council of the United Nations that land reform in the backward countries must be "the whole basis of development," and he has never hesitated to advocate careful economic planning—a concept not usually popular among American financiers, who tend to suppose that what was good for General Motors is good for Wulustan. The Bank is unexpectedly liberal in some of its attitudes, and it is precisely the paradoxical union of orthodoxy and vision that has made it so much respected alike in Leopoldville and Cedar Rapids.

But in its present form it cannot always honor these advanced principles, for the reasons we have examined: and if we imagine the silhouette of this institution outlined against the future, we shall perhaps see it overshadowed by a recent affiliate, the International Development Association, which shares President, staff, offices, and values with the World Bank but is specifically designed to take a step further forward. It lends money on much easier terms to countries less formally suitable for loans, but for projects vetted just as carefully as ever. Because it does not go to the private market for its funds, but depends upon the munificence of member governments, IDA can be gentler in its stipulations. It can put money into things not commercially profitable, like education and pure water. It can be more lenient about terms of repayment. (It normally allows a ten-year period of grace, when nothing need be paid back at all, and then another forty years on what the British call the never-never and the Irish, with their gift for liquid euphemism, the "gradual payments scheme.") Most important of all, IDA charges no interest:

the only cost to the borrower is a service charge to cover the administrative costs.

Some of the Bank's critics resent the fact that this new organism should come under the control of H Street at all, but many others have been appeased by this open-handed chip off the old block. It is a sign of confidence, rather than of compromise, for it proves that the Bank, having laboriously established its reputation for stability and conventional business sense, now feels strong enough to explore some more adventurous attitudes. IDA has cheerfully shouldered numbers of loans that would not appeal to its snootier parent, and many people at H Street foresee the day when it will outstrip the Bank in scale as in imagination. Its very emergence is a kind of image of developing philosophies—from the rigidity of whole-hog, profit-making, unbending capitalism to something more flexible, more generous, and (*pace* the Capitol Hill zealots) more free.

The present snag is that since IDA, by the nature of its operations, cannot raise funds privately, it has very little money. The World Bank is limitlessly rich, but short of the clients to which, as the upstage mamas used to say, it has become accustomed: the International Development Association has customers on every corner, but scarcely a sou to offer them. Visionaries foresee a day, though, when the member governments of Bank and Association will be willing to abandon the arid competition of bilateral aid and channel all their funds for the emergent nations, loans and gifts as well, through the skilled and universally respected machineries of H Street. Far from being marginal or catalytic, as the work of the World Bank has so far been, this would then be the

The Road to Huddersfield:

very vortex of the world's development, the anvil on which all the new Huddersfields are forged, a center of hope and advice and support to which the poor nations, east and west, could always look for the tempered and cool-eyed generosity they have a right to expect.

For myself, I like to imagine this new World Bank as the seed of something greater still, for it seems to me in my more starry-eyed moments to have a potentially messianic quality, gruff but golden. I find it difficult to believe that up on the East River, where the little men squabble the debates away and the big ones posture incessantly upon the rostrum, the United Nations will ever mature into a world government: it lacks the fiber, the discipline, the command, the strong hand. In 1818 H Street, though, it is not hard to envisage the nucleus of a properly international civil service, dedicated not just to the dispersal of money but to the development of the world's welfare in the fullest sense—just as the Bank's Development Advisory Service already forms the cadre of an international technical corps. The tradition of integrity and detachment is there already, the experience of dealing with almost every class and character of nation, the reputation built up contract by contract, project by project, loan by loan, over a decade and a half of dogged equity. Could such an instrument one day convince even the Communists that charity is the common duty of us all? Could it persuade even the wildest of the true-blue senators that the world is not irreparably split in hostility? Could it bring a new decency and dignity to the Huddersfield road? Could it really work? Would it really last?

I like to think it might, and sometimes I dare to imagine,

when I walk the chill hygienic purlieus of 1818 H Street, that somewhere among those gray walls I can descry, as I wobble past the trim, tight secretaries, stagger giddily through the jargon, evade the worst of the patronizing bores and pretend to read the newest thesis on the Prospective Demand for and Supply of Non-Agricultural Commodities over the Medium Term—as I hasten shamefaced toward the Infra-Reddy coffee machine, I like to pretend I can make out, as through a plastic veil, the dim lineaments of Blake's new Zion.

But we can get there only through the satanic mills, via Leeds and Slaithwaite, Oldham and Crosland. Our Yorkshire archetype has long been overtaken, and it is no longer to those grim, blackened valleys that the aspirant peoples look when they dream of ingots and ball-bearings. England herself, that brassiest pioneer of steam, has been left behind in the age of electronics, just as Holland, for so many generations the leader of western progress, found herself too exhausted to lead the Industrial Revolution. Still, Huddersfield people have lived longest of all in the company of the machine, and it is to Huddersfield that we will return at last, to see what hope or misery she offers.

Do not be despondent as the street lamps flicker sadly on and you turn up your collar against that steely moorland wind. Poor Susan is long since reconciled. Huddersfield has suffered indeed for her priority among the machine cities—suffered with mean, dank houses, warped young limbs, ugliness, and rotted lungs. Nearly two centuries have passed, though, since she reached that moment of harsh exuberance—that Take-off, that Illumination of Choices, that Application of Science and

The Road to Huddersfield:

Savings. She has mellowed and stretched her limbs since then, and grown out of her brutalities. She will never be a patrician sort of place, for all her mill-owners' Rolls-Royces. She is not stylish or open-handed—"a middling stinter," is how Yorkshiremen describe her. She has developed over the decades a parochial complacency that is often irritating and sometimes ludicrous: you can buy *Oggi* or *Paris Match* in her streets any afternoon, but this is Yorkshire, lad, and you still can't buy the Manchester evening papers. She lacks the finesse of Bangkok, say, the nobility of Addis, the cultivation of Bogota, the sizzle of Cagliari, even the martial swagger of Rawalpindi, astrut with bugle calls and epaulets above the Indus Basin.

But there, her prides and snobberies are straightforward enough, based as they are upon hard cash and the state of the drapes, and she has a keen, straight eye for quality, fair trading, and square deals. You still have to push in Huddersfield, but nobody will much care whether your arm is black, brown, or grubby white, your creed Christian, Muslim, or conventionally pagan. Once no more than a shudder in a fastidious mind or a pang in a homesick bosom, Huddersfield now commands fierce loyalties and affectionate respect. Many a poshly educated young man, sent away to expensive boarding school, soon reverts to his Huddersfield brogue when he returns to Chapel Hill for the holidays.

She is shabby still, but not heartless, for she has virtually eliminated poverty and illiteracy. She is a town rich in choral societies and brass bands, the Invalid Tricycle Club, the Rough Stuff Fellowship, the noisy young Luddites on their motorcycles. She is a town of deep stability, where a panic is difficult to conceive, and a crust of blunt pessimism barely disguises an unshakable self-confidence. She is seldom vulgar, curmudgeonly, or ostentatious. She no longer feels *nouveau riche*. She is, in short, no longer an exciting or a provocative place, but she has evolved a society that is, as human institutions go, strong, decent, and kindly.

So she looks, nearly two centuries after the event, and this is a comfort: for as we have seen, the revolution that started in these northern valleys, and is still fizzling and erupting in all the continents of the earth, is not always pleasant in its origins. Huddersfield offers us a last reassurance. In Cairo or Kiruna, in the mines of Mauretania or the Indian steel towns, they need no longer look toward her with envy, but they can draw upon her for encouragement. The cruelty, she seems to say, need not be permanent. The degradation will not last.

All this you will see clearly if you rub your sense of history: but if you do not have it handy, then the dusk will fall like a damp blanket over Huddersfield, the soot will dirty your collar and clog your nostrils, the coffee-shop door will slam in your face, and you will pity from the bottom of your heart those poor, ignorant innocents, the world over, who pine to exchange their pastorals for the blast of the foundries and the clatter of engines in the half-light.

No. AM00000

INTERNATIONAL BANK FOR RECONSTRUCTION AND DEVELOPMENT

$1000   **$1000**

Ten Year Canadian Dollar Bond of 1952,
Due February 1, 1962
4%

INTERNATIONAL BANK FOR RECONSTRUCTION AND DEVELOPMENT, an international institution established by Articles of Agreement among the respective Governments signatory thereto (hereinafter called the Bank), for value received, hereby promises to pay to the bearer hereof, on the first day of February, 1962, or on such earlier date as the principal sum may become payable in accordance with the provisions hereof, at any agency of the Bank of Canada in Canada, at the holder's option, the sum of

ONE THOUSAND DOLLARS

in lawful money of Canada, and to pay interest thereon from the date hereof at any of said agencies, at the holder's option, in like money at the rate of four per centum (4%) per annum, payable semi-annually on August 1, 1952, and on each February 1 and August 1 thereafter until payment of said principal sum has been made or duly provided for, but until the maturity hereof only upon presentation and surrender of the coupons thereto attached as they severally mature.

This Bond is one of an authorized issue of bonds of the aggregate principal amount of $15,000,000, known as the Ten Year Canadian Dollar Bonds of 1952, due February 1, 1962, of the Bank (hereinafter called the Bonds).

The Bank covenants that, so long as any of the Bonds shall be outstanding and unpaid, the Bank will not cause or permit to be created on any of its property or assets any mortgage, pledge or other lien or charge as security for any bonds or other evidences of indebtedness heretofore or hereafter issued, assumed or guaranteed by the Bank for money borrowed (other than purchase money mortgages, pledges or liens on property purchased by the Bank as security for all or part of the purchase price thereof), unless the Bonds shall be secured by such mortgage, pledge or other lien or charge equally and ratably with such other bonds or evidences of indebtedness.

If the Bank shall default in the payment of the principal of, or interest on, or in the performance of any covenant in respect of a sinking fund in, any of the Bonds or any other bonds or similar obligations hereafter issued, assumed or guaranteed by the Bank and such default shall continue for a period of 90 days, then at any time thereafter and during the continuance of such default the holder of any of the Bonds may deliver or cause to be delivered to the Bank at its principal office in the City of Washington, District of Columbia, United States of America, written notice that such holder elects to declare the principal of all Bonds held by him (the serial numbers and denominations of which shall be set forth in such notice) to be due and payable, and on the thirtieth day after such notice shall have been so delivered to the Bank the principal of such Bonds shall become due and payable, unless prior to that time all such defaults theretofore existing shall have been cured.

Upon payment, if the Bank shall so require, of a charge calculated to reimburse the Bank for the cost of the exchange or transfer, including any tax or other governmental charge connected therewith: (1) bearer Bonds with interest coupons attached (herein called coupon Bonds) may be exchanged upon presentation and surrender thereof at the Bank of Canada, for coupon Bonds of other authorized denominations, or for fully registered Bonds without coupons (herein called registered Bonds) of any authorized denominations, or both, in the same aggregate principal amount; (2) registered Bonds may be exchanged upon presentation and surrender at the Bank of Canada, in Ottawa, Canada, for registered Bonds of other authorized denominations or for coupon Bonds of any authorized denominations, or both, in the same aggregate principal amount and (3) any registered Bond may be transferred by the registered holder thereof, or by his attorney duly authorized in writing, at the Bank of Canada, in Ottawa, Canada, upon presentation and surrender of such Bond for cancellation, and upon any such transfer a new registered Bond or Bonds, of authorized denominations and in the same aggregate principal amount, will be issued to the transferee.

The Bank shall not be required to make transfers or exchanges of (1) any Bonds during a period of twenty days next preceding any interest payment date or (2) any Bonds called for redemption.

Coupon Bonds which shall be presented and surrendered by the holders thereof, or delivered by or on behalf of the Bank, pursuant to the provisions hereof, shall be accompanied by all coupons thereto appertaining which shall not have matured on or before the date of such presentation and surrender or delivery, as the case may be, except that, in the case of Bonds so presented and surrendered, or delivered, for purposes of redemption, such Bonds shall be accompanied by all coupons thereto appertaining which shall not have matured on or before the redemption date. All registered Bonds which shall be presented and surrendered pursuant to the provisions hereof shall be duly endorsed or accompanied by a proper instrument or instruments of assignment and transfer.

As a sinking fund for the Bonds, until all the Bonds shall have been purchased or paid and retired or shall have become due, the Bank will retire on or before February 1 of each of the years 1955 to 1960, both inclusive, not less than $700,000 principal amount of the Bonds and on or before February 1, 1961, not less than $800,000 principal amount of the Bonds.

The Bank shall have the right to apply in satisfaction of its sinking fund obligations Bonds, to the extent of the principal amount thereof, previously purchased or redeemed (otherwise than for such purpose). No Bonds shall be issued to operate in substitution for the principal amount of Bonds retired for sinking fund purposes.

The Bonds are subject to redemption at the election of the Bank, as follows:

(a) In an aggregate principal amount not exceeding $700,000 in each period of twelve months ending February 1 of the years 1955 to 1960, both inclusive, and $800,000 in the twelve months ending February 1, 1961, at a redemption price for each Bond or, as to any Bond of a denomination in excess of $1,000 not all of which is to be redeemed, for the portion thereof to be redeemed, equal to the principal amount thereof to be redeemed, plus the interest accrued and unpaid thereon to the date fixed for the redemption thereof, and

(b) As a whole at any time or in part from time to time for the portion thereof to be redeemed, equal to the principal amount thereof to be redeemed, plus the interest accrued and unpaid thereon to the date fixed for the redemption thereof, plus a premium the following respective percentages of such principal amount: 2%, if the redemption date shall be on or before January 31, 1954; 1½%, if the redemption date shall be thereafter and on or before January 31, 1956; 1%, if the redemption date shall be thereafter and on or before January 31, 1958; ½%, if the redemption date shall be thereafter and on or before January 31, 1960, and without premium, if the redemption date shall be thereafter.

In case of any partial redemption, the Bonds to be redeemed shall be selected by lot by the Bank.

Notice of any redemption of Bonds it shall give notice of its intention to redeem and the Bonds, or part of the Bonds selected as hereinbefore provided, as the case may be. Such notice of redemption shall designate the redemption date and the redemption price, determined as hereinbefore provided, and, unless all the outstanding Bonds are to be redeemed, the designating numbers and principal amount of the Bonds which are to be redeemed and in case any Bond is to be redeemed in part only, the principal amount thereof to be redeemed. Such notice shall be given by publication in a daily newspaper, printed in the English language and published and of general circulation in each of the cities of Montreal, Ottawa and Toronto, and in a daily newspaper printed in the French language and published in the City of Montreal, at least three times prior to said redemption date, the first publication to be not less than 45 nor more than 60 days prior to said redemption date and shall be mailed not less than 45 nor more than 60 days prior to said redemption date to each holder of registered Bonds at his last address appearing on the books of the Bank. Accidental error or omission in giving notice to any bondholder shall not invalidate or otherwise prejudicially affect the redemption of the Bonds to be redeemed. Notice of redemption having been given as above provided, the Bonds or portions thereof so called for redemption shall become due and payable on said redemption date at the redemption price and, upon presentation and surrender thereof, on or after such date, at any agency of the Bank of Canada in Canada, at the holder's option, shall be paid at the redemption price aforesaid. All unpaid interest represented by coupons which shall have matured on or prior to said redemption date shall continue to be payable to the bearers of such coupons severally and respectively, and the redemption price payable to the holders of coupon Bonds presented for redemption shall not include such interest except to the extent that such coupons shall accompany such Bonds. From and after said redemption date, if payment is duly made or provided for, the Bonds or portions thereof so called for redemption shall cease to bear interest and any appurtenant coupons maturing after said redemption date shall be void; provided, however, that, if any Bond shall be of a denomination in excess of $1,000, and a portion only of the principal amount thereof shall be so called for redemption, the Bank shall upon presentation and surrender of such Bond issue and deliver, without charge to the holder, a new registered Bond or Bonds, or a new coupon Bond or Bonds, in an aggregate principal amount equal to the portion of the principal amount of such Bond not so called for redemption.

The Bank may deem and treat the bearer of any coupon Bond, and the bearer of any coupon thereof, and the person in whose name any registered Bond shall be registered on the books of the Bank, as the absolute owner thereof for all purposes whatsoever notwithstanding any notice to the contrary; and all payments to such bearer or to or in the order of such registered owner, as the case may be, shall be valid and effectual to discharge the liability of the Bank upon such coupon Bond, such coupon or such registered Bond to the extent of the sum or sums so paid.

No recourse shall be had for the payment of the principal of, or the interest on, this Bond or any part thereof, or for any claim based hereon or otherwise in respect hereof or of the indebtedness represented hereby or by the coupons appertaining hereto, against any governor or executive director, or alternate of either, or against any officer or employee, as such, past, present or future, of the Bank or of any successor to the Bank, whether by virtue of any constitutional provision, statute or rule of law, or by the enforcement of any assessment or penalty or otherwise, all such liability being by the acceptance hereof and as part of the consideration for the issue hereof expressly waived and released.

This Bond shall not be valid or become obligatory for any purpose until it shall have been authenticated by the certificate of Bank of Canada, or its successor, as Fiscal Agent, hereon endorsed.

THIS BOND IS NOT AN OBLIGATION OF ANY GOVERNMENT.

IN WITNESS WHEREOF, the Bank has caused this Bond to be signed in its name with the facsimile signature of its President and of its Treasurer and its official seal to be hereto affixed, or a facsimile thereof to be printed or engraved hereon, and to be attested with the facsimile signature of its Secretary, and the coupons for said interest bearing the facsimile signature of its Treasurer to be attached hereto.

Dated February 1, 1952.

International Bank for Reconstruction and Development

SPECIMEN

Attest:

M. Mendels
Secretary

Eugene R. Black
President

[signature]
Treasurer